30-Minute Groups

GROUPS

LIFE SKILLS

INCREASING EMPATHY, BUILDING RESILIENCE, AND MANAGING SELF

ELiSHiA BASNER

NATIONAL CENTER for YOUTH ISSUES

Duplication and Copyright

No part of this publication may be reproduced, stored in a retrieval system, or transmitted in any form by any means, electronic, mechanical, photocopy, video or audio recording, or otherwise without prior written permission from the publisher, except for all worksheets and activities which may be reproduced for a specific group or class. Reproduction for an entire school or school district is prohibited.

NCYI titles may be purchased in bulk at special discounts for educational, business, fundraising, or promotional use. For more information, please email sales@ncyi.org.

NATIONAL CENTER for YOUTH ISSUES
P.O. Box 22185
Chattanooga, TN 37422-2185
423.899.5714 • 866.318.6294
fax: 423.899.4547 • www.ncyi.org

ISBN: 9781953945860
© 2024 National Center for Youth Issues, Chattanooga, TN
All rights reserved.
Written by: Elishia Basner
Published by National Center for Youth Issues
Printed in the U.S.A. • August 2025

Third party links are accurate at the time of publication, but may change over time.

The information in this book is designed to provide helpful information on the subjects discussed and is not intended to be used, nor should it be used, to diagnose or treat any mental health or medical condition. For diagnosis or treatment of any mental health or medical issue, consult a licensed counselor, psychologist, or physician. The publisher and author are not responsible for any specific mental or physical health needs that may require medical supervision, and are not liable for any damages or negative consequences from any treatment, action, application, or preparation, to any person reading or following the information in this book. References are provided for informational purposes only and do not constitute endorsement of any websites or other sources.

ASCA National Model®, Recognized ASCA Model Program® and RAMP® are registered trademarks of the American School Counselor Association. Our use of them does not imply an affiliation with or endorsement by the American School Counselor Association.

Contents

Introduction 4
    What's Included 4
    Accompanying Group Documents 5

Introductory Group Session 7

Chapter 1: Kindness 8

Chapter 2: Patience 14

Chapter 3: Respect 21

Chapter 4: Gratitude 27

Chapter 5: Responsibility 33

Chapter 6: Honesty 40

Chapter 7: Friendship 47

Chapter 8: Compassion 53

Chapter 9: Forgiveness 59

Chapter 10: Perseverance 65

Final Group Session 72

Downloadable Resources 72

Small Group Action Plan Guide 73

Life Skills Group Permission Form 74

Life Skills Group Expectations 75

Group Attendance Form 76

Group Attendance Form (Example) 77

Pre- and Post-Group Survey 78

Post-Group Survey Results 79

Post-Group Survey Results (Example) 80

Certificate of Completion 81

Life Skills Group Completion Letter 82

References 83

About the Author 83

About NCYI 84

Introduction

Good life skills give children the confidence to make healthy decisions and build strong relationships with peers and adults. This Life Skills curriculum consists of ten to twelve thirty-minute sessions to help students learn the skills necessary to make healthy decisions, build strong relationships, develop better problem-solving and communication skills, and manage their emotions in difficult situations. Our goal with this curriculum is to help children become more well-rounded individuals and handle life's challenges with resilience and determination.

This Life Skills curriculum is tailored for 2nd through 8th graders and covers essential topics such as kindness, patience, respect, gratitude, responsibility, honesty, friendship, compassion, forgiveness, and perseverance. While some of these topics may seem obvious, it's often the first time someone has explicitly taught the students you are working with this information. This curriculum recognizes the unique ways in which each student learns, emphasizing that there's no singular 'correct' way to embrace these ideas. Just as each lesson is individualized to cater to diverse learning styles, the curriculum remains flexible, ensuring that every child can engage, understand, and practice these essential life skills.

The strategic design allows students to empathize, connect with others, and translate their new knowledge into practice. The American School Counselor Association (ASCA®)-aligned curriculum contains an introductory lesson, ten core Life Skills lessons, and a final closing lesson. Facilitators have the flexibility to include the initial and final lessons as part of the core sessions if they have extra time.

You'll find a range of essential resources in the book's concluding pages. These consist of permission and completion letters, attendance logs, a group expectation form, and a certificate of completion. You'll also find pre- and post-group surveys to measure the success of the programming and templates to share the results with interested parties. Moreover, this workbook provides a comprehensive small group action plan that will integrate effortlessly into your ASCA® evaluation document and facilitate a seamless transition from planning to assessment.

Practical and applicable, the activities provided are suitable for small and large group instruction and require no additional materials. You do not need to bring supplies beyond pencils, markers or crayons, and scratch paper; you won't need to spend hours prepping materials before meeting with your students. Everything you need is included!

See Page 72 for information on Downloadable Resources

What's Included:

Life Skills: Comprises ten lessons and all necessary documents to conduct a group. Following the overview of the lesson curriculum, you'll find supporting documentation to develop a small group within the school setting.

Mind Map: Provides an illustrated diagram of the life skill that can help students make connections between the life skill and other concepts. Students should begin each lesson by considering the meaning of the specific life skill. It is optional to write these, but visuals are helpful for many students. Some have found it helpful to draw the Mind Map on the board, or you can draw a tree with the life skill written on the trunk and the related words on the fruit on the tree.

ASCA® Standards: Each lesson includes success criteria for the learning target.

Lesson Introduction: At the start of each lesson, we will introduce a concept and explain it to provide clarity for the upcoming story.

Circle Time Questions: This section has three optional questions for the facilitator to start the conversation. These questions allow students to deepen their understanding of the topic and build community by discussing and sharing their experiences.

Story Time: Provides stories related to the life skill that should be read aloud to help children understand the concept.

Coloring Sheets: Allow students to visualize the life skill. Students can color the sheet while the facilitator shares the initial story after the lesson is complete or take it home with them.

Discussion Questions: Students can discuss the questions posed to help them process their beliefs on the subject.

Skill Practice/How Would You Practice ___ Skill If?: Using the round-robin method, go around the table and ask students how they would practice that skill, giving them each a chance to answer one question.

Additional Activities: Provides activities to help students practice and apply the concept.

Closing Considerations: Is an opportunity to review the concept and ask students to reflect on their new experience with the material.

Would You Rather? Game: Provides an opportunity for students to consider what they would "rather" do related to the lesson's topic. The facilitator can cut out the cards and let students discuss or read aloud while moving from one side of the room to the other to communicate their preferred answer.

Accompanying Group Documents:

Small Group Action Plan Guide: Provides the necessary information required to complete the ASCA® National Model's Small Group Action Plan.

Permission Form: The permission form is used to gain the permission of the student's caregivers for the child to attend the Life Skills group. Be sure to send this home about two weeks before the group starts.

Group Expectations: These provide basic expectations for the group process. The form has space for the facilitator and group to collaborate on adding additional expectations to fit their group.

Group Attendance Form: This is a blank form that allows the facilitator to track which students attended each session and what topics were discussed.

Group Attendance Form (Example): This form is an example of how to best utilize the group attendance form.

Pre- and Post-Group Survey: Provides an opportunity for students to share what they know of the concepts before and after they've completed the curriculum.

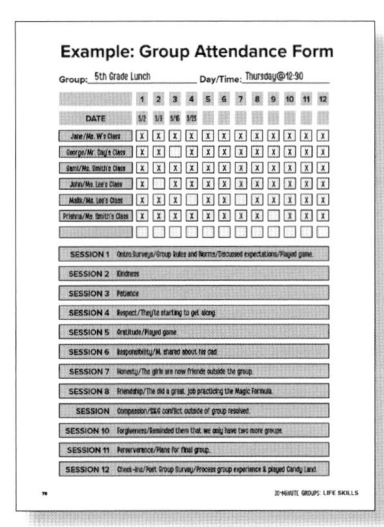

To measure the progress of students who participate, use the same assessment for both the pre-group and post-group survey. Administer the pre-group survey at the start of the instructional period, followed by instruction and practice opportunities for measured skills or knowledge.

At the end of the instructional period, administer the post-survey and compare the results of both surveys to identify areas of improvement and areas that need further instruction. Then calculate the average score of the pre-survey and post-survey and determine the percentage of improvement by subtracting the pre-survey average from the post-survey average and then dividing the result by the pre-survey average. Use this pre-survey average improvement to measure the students' progress effectively.

Percentage of Improvement Formula:
((Post-Group Total - Pre-Group Total) / Pre-Group Total)) x 100 = Percentage of Overall Improvement

Example:
((44 Post Group Total - 31 Pre-Group Total) / 31) x 100 = 41.94% Overall Improvement

Look at your data to determine who should attend your group. Review conduct referrals, attendance data, and achievement metrics and look for students with deficits. Consider also tracking students' academic achievements, absences, and discipline referrals. You can better see the impact of your small groups when strategically selecting students and closely monitoring their academic, attendance, and conduct metrics. Be sure to share the results of your intervention with your advisory council.

Post-Group Survey Results: The survey shows one way to share your data with your interested parties. Remember, we want to make sure that we use graphs and charts as they show our data, which is often more impactful than a paragraph of text. Use whatever platform you prefer to show your data but be sure to complete the data following the group and then share with your interested parties.

Post-Group Survey Results (Example): The survey shows what your data might resemble following the completion of the groups. You can use this form to share your data.

Certificate of Completion: Present students with a certificate to congratulate them on completing the curriculum.

Life Skills Group Completion Letter: Letter written to the caregivers/guardians of students following the completion of the group. Provide students with their certificate and their life skills group review letter during the last session.

Additional Materials: We promised to provide everything you need in this workbook, and we have. However, you will need to make copies of the pre- and post-group assessment surveys and print the coloring pages. You might also print and cut the "Would You Rather?" game or facilitate that activity verbally. We recommend having crayons or colored pencils readily available on the table for those who wish to complete the coloring sheet. It might also be helpful to have some fidgets accessible for your students during their group session.

Good luck with your group! We hope you have a fantastic experience!

Introductory Group Session

Directions & Overview

Conducting this introductory session is recommended but not required, as the content covered here can easily integrate into the first core Life Skills session, especially if there's additional time during your first meeting. You have the flexibility to initiate the group activities at your convenience once you've analyzed your data to identify appropriate participants and obtained their caregiver permission forms.

Directions: We recommend that you meet with the students to complete this introductory group session before conducting the first lesson. You will start by welcoming all of the students to the group. Then, explain the group's purpose and instill hope for gaining new knowledge and having fun together!

Survey: Before you progress further, read the instructions for the pre-group survey to the students. Discreetly review the forms as they are given to you to ensure that each question has been answered.

Introductions: Help your students get to know one another by asking them to share their names, something about themselves, and what they hope to learn from the group. Explain that during each session, they will be asked to share a highlight and lowlight for the week or check in using the weather to represent their emotions in a small group format. Offer to practice that check-in now.

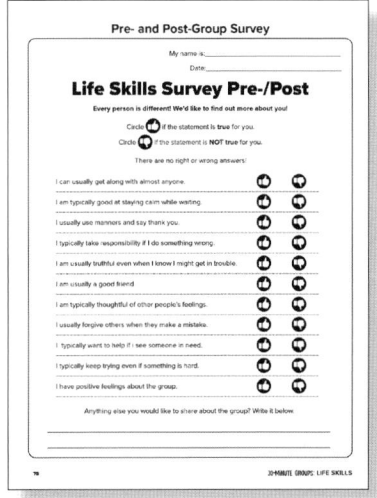

Explain the Group Format: Explain where and how often you will meet. Share the list of topics. Explain that, in each meeting, you'll discuss one of the topics together, then read a story, and answer questions. Discuss the logistics of what they'll do while you are reading; they'll be eating (if it is a lunch group) or completing their coloring sheet. Explain that they'll have time to work in pairs for the Skill Practice portion and play a "Would You Rather?" game. Finally, explain that at the end of each session, they'll be asked to give a one-sentence overview of what they've learned and make a plan to practice that lesson topic throughout the week.

Review Group Expectations: Print a copy of the Group Expectations. Review the expectations together with the students and answer questions as they arise. Take time to collaborate with your group to determine whether you need to modify or add expectations.

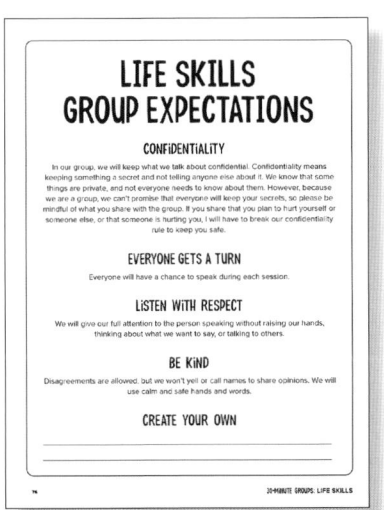

Group Conclusion: Ask each student to summarize the information they learned from this session into one sentence. Students may share with their partners or the group.

Note to Facilitators: You can customize the material to fit the needs of your group. If your students are not yet readers, you can read the "Would You Rather?" game questions aloud and request that students move to different sides of the room to show their answers. If you're working with shy students, they can write their responses to questions instead of sharing them aloud or break into smaller teams to discuss. Some facilitators may choose to incorporate traditional games into the lessons if they have longer session times. Remember, the workbook is just the framework, but you will bring it to life!

Kindness

> **KINDNESS:** *a kind nature; being kind rather than doing harm; gentle; a kind act.*

MIND MAP

On the board, draw a mind map and ask students to consider the meaning of *kindness*.

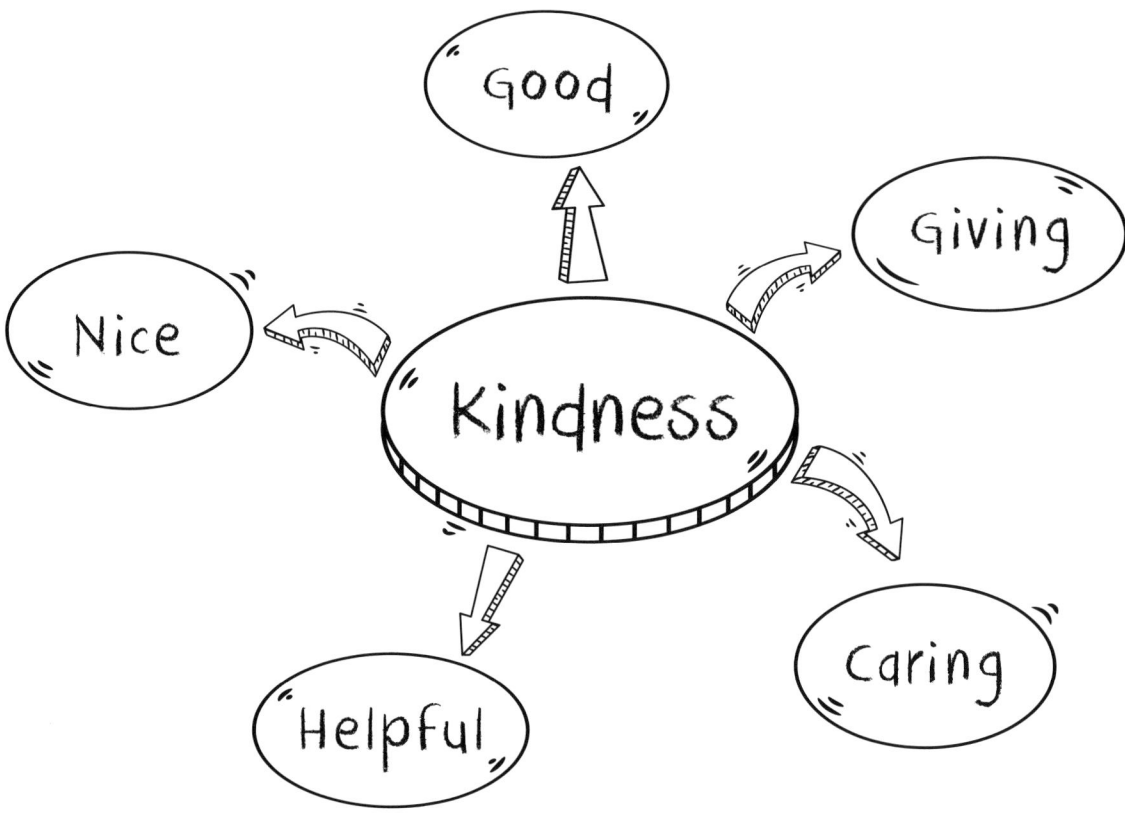

ASCA® STANDARDS

- **B-SS 2.** Positive, respectful, and supportive relationships with students who are similar to and different from them.
- **B-SS 4.** Empathy.
- **B-SS 10.** Cultural awareness, sensitivity, and responsiveness.

DIRECTIONS

Prior to the first group, be sure your students have completed the Pre-/Post-Group Survey. In a small group format, complete a brief check-in with your students by asking them to share a highlight and lowlight for the week or by using the weather to represent their emotions. In a large group format, you might ask for a thumb up if they're feeling good, a thumb sideways in the middle if they're feeling okay, and a thumb down if they aren't doing well. Review the Group Expectations before reviewing the Mind Map. Then, read the Lesson Introduction and ask the Circle Time Questions before reading the Story and asking the Discussion Questions. Students can work in pairs to craft their responses or share with the whole group. Complete the Skill Practice, "Would You Rather?" game, and Additional Activities as time allows. Be sure to complete the Closing Considerations with each lesson.

LESSON INTRODUCTION

Kindness is being thoughtful, friendly, or generous. We can show kindness by writing thank-you letters to show appreciation, helping around the house, giving compliments, or even smiling at our classmates. Kindness is treating others how you'd want to be treated. When we are kind, it can make others feel good, and they want to spread their kindness to other people.

CIRCLE TIME QUESTIONS

Ask students to reflect and share their answers to the following questions with the group. Larger groups may need to be broken into smaller groups to give students ample time to share their answers and deepen the conversation.

- Can you think of a time in your life when someone was kind to you?
- What is your favorite way to show kindness to others?
- Can you think of a time when you wanted to be kind to someone but didn't follow through? Share how you felt about that experience.

STORY TIME

Hand out coloring sheets and crayons or markers to students to work on while the facilitator reads the story, if desired.

Kindness Can Be Contagious

Shana was Blue Bear Middle School's newest student. She'd been there a week and had made no friends. She was super friendly, played the drums, and was amazing at math and science, but most kids had barely looked at her since she'd arrived. Shana was diagnosed as a baby with a rare bone disease and could not use her legs, so she used a wheelchair to get around. Her classmates had never met anyone in a wheelchair and weren't sure what to say or how to act when she was around, so they kept their distance.

Sam, one of her classmates, noticed she hadn't made any friends yet. One night after school, Sam mentioned Shana to his dad and told him he was nervous about trying to make friends with her. Sam asked, "What if I say something stupid and hurt her feelings?" Sam's dad asked, "Can you remember what it felt like when we moved here, and you were the new kid?" Sam shuddered; he remembered he'd been so nervous that his palms were sweaty, and his stomach felt like it was doing flips. "Yeah," he replied, "I was doing breathing exercises for most of the first day just to stay calm enough to hear the teacher." His dad smiled, "And do you remember what else helped you feel calmer?" Sam's face broke into a big grin. "I do. The guys asked me to play soccer with them at recess." His dad gave him a knowing look, and Sam realized that even though he was nervous about making friends with Shana, she must be way more nervous than him.

The next day, Sam got up the courage to smile at Shana during breakfast and give her a little wave. It was a small gesture of kindness, but she smiled and waved back. Then at lunch, he invited Shana to have lunch with him and introduced her to his friends. Many of their classmates had been worried that they wouldn't have anything in common with Shana, so they'd avoided her, but when they saw Sam spending time with her, they realized that even though she got around differently, she was a kid just like them. It wasn't long before Shana had made many friends, and at the end of the year, Shana, Sam, and four of their classmates won the school's talent show due in no small part to Shana's excellent drumming skills.

DISCUSSION QUESTIONS

- What was the first act of kindness Sam showed to Shana?
- Why was Sam nervous to make friends with Shana?
- What are a few acts of kindness that can brighten someone's day?
- How did Sam's example of kindness help his classmates become Shana's friends?
- If you were Sam, what might have held you back from trying to make friends with someone new?

SKILL PRACTICE

Using the round-robin method, go around the table and ask students how they would practice each skill, giving everyone a chance to answer one question. Skill Practice can be adapted to allow students to answer in pairs or write their answers on scratch paper.

How Would You Practice Kindness If:

- Your grownup is trying to fix dinner but is not feeling well?
- Your little brother is feeling sad because he received a low grade on his spelling test?
- A friend falls off her bike and skins her knee?
- You notice one of your classmates playing alone at recess?
- During a baseball game, your best friend strikes out?
- A new student comes into your class and doesn't know anyone?
- A classmate is being teased because of a birthmark on his face?
- It's your teacher's birthday?
- Your friend dropped their hoodie in the mud?
- Your baby sister is pulling the cat's tail?

ADDITIONAL ACTIVITIES

- Divide the group into pairs. Ask each student to share a story with their partner about a time in their life when they practiced being kind. Then, ask each person to retell their partner's story.
- Ask students to write five different ways in which they will try to practice acts of kindness over the next several days. Then, in the next session, have them take out their paper and discuss their progress with the group.

CLOSING CONSIDERATIONS

A kind person is thoughtful of others and themselves. Kindness is not something we have to do; being kind is a choice that is sometimes difficult to make, but often feels good. When we are kind to others, we treat them how we want to be treated.

Ask students to summarize the content of this session's lesson into a single sentence. Students will then consider how they will practice kindness throughout the next week. In pairs or groups of three, students may share their answers. If time allows, a few students may share with the whole group.

"WOULD YOU RATHER?" GAME

Playing the "Would You Rather?" game is a fun and engaging activity for students to develop their critical thinking skills. Students will reflect on their experience, evaluate their options based on their preferences, and reflect on the opinions of others, providing a different perspective and strengthening their sense of connection to one another.

Would You Rather?

Copy and cut out the questions for small groups to discuss, or have each person stand in the center of the room and move towards one side or the other to show their vote for either option as the facilitator reads the questions aloud.

- WOULD YOU RATHER BE GIVEN $10 TO BUY YOUR GROWNUP A GIFT OR GIVEN $10 FOR YOURSELF?

- WOULD YOU RATHER HOLD THE DOOR OPEN FOR THE PERSON BEHIND YOU OR LET IT SLAM ON THEM?

- WOULD YOU RATHER HELP A FRIEND WITH THEIR SCHOOLWORK OR PRETEND YOU DIDN'T HEAR THEM ASK FOR HELP?

- WOULD YOU RATHER DONATE YOUR OLD CLOTHES TO CHARITY OR KEEP THEM FOR YOURSELF?

- WOULD YOU RATHER SMILE AT A CLASSMATE WHO IS HAVING A BAD DAY OR NOT LOOK IN THEIR DIRECTION?

- WOULD YOU RATHER PICK UP LITTER YOU SEE IN THE HALLWAY OR IGNORE IT AND KEEP WALKING?

30-MINUTE GROUPS: LIFE SKILLS

> *"I've learned that people will forget what you said, people will forget what you did, but people will never forget how you made them feel."*
>
> MAYA ANGELOU

KINDNESS

30-MINUTE GROUPS: LIFE SKILLS

PATIENCE

[*PATIENCE: a willingness to put up with waiting, pain, or trouble; a calm bearing of anything that annoys or hurts.*]

MIND MAP

On the board, draw a mind map and ask students to consider the meaning of *patience*.

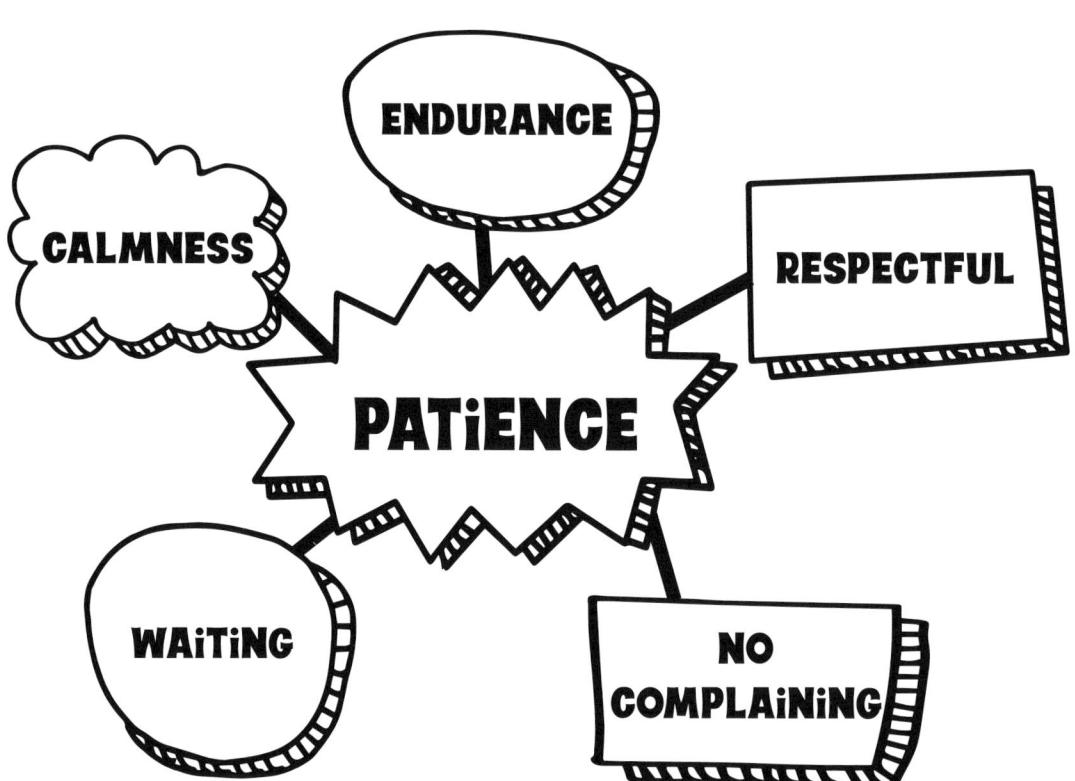

ASCA® STANDARDS

- **B-SMS 2.** Self-discipline and self-control.
- **B-SMS 4.** Delayed gratification for long-term rewards.

DIRECTIONS

In a small group format, complete a brief check-in with your students by asking them to share a highlight and lowlight for the week or by using the weather to represent their emotions. In a large group format, you might ask for a thumb up if they're feeling good, a thumb in the middle if they're feeling okay, or a thumb down if they aren't doing well. Review the Group Expectations before asking students to share their knowledge of the topic from the previous session. Together, review the Mind Map. Then, read the Lesson Introduction and ask the Circle Time Questions before reading the Story and asking the Discussion Questions. Students can work in pairs to craft their responses or share with the whole group. Complete the Skill Practice, "Would You Rather?" game, and Additional Activities as time allows. Be sure to complete the Closing Considerations with each lesson.

LESSON INTRODUCTION

Patience is the ability to wait without getting upset or angry. Patience is accepting a delay in your plans without complaining or whining. Patience is also working toward future goals consistently and continuing to try, even when things are difficult. We can practice patience when waiting in line, to be called on in class, or for someone else to finish speaking. Even when things don't go as planned, when we can stay calm, it allows us to think clearly and make kind and thoughtful choices.

Waiting for your turn and being patient takes practice and can help you develop self-control. Self-control is necessary to help you accomplish your future goals and dreams. It is important to remember that everyone's brain works differently, and patience comes easier to some of us than others.

CIRCLE TIME QUESTIONS

Ask students to reflect and share their answers to the following questions with the group. Larger groups may need to be broken into smaller groups to give students ample time to share their answers and deepen the conversation.

- What situations make you feel most impatient? (Waiting in line, walking behind someone moving slowly, etc.)
- What are some physical signs that someone might be feeling impatient? (Foot tapping, sighing, glaring, etc.)
- What are some strategies you use to help you be more patient? (Breathing, distracting yourself, etc.)

30-MINUTE GROUPS: **LIFE SKILLS**

STORY TIME

Hand out coloring sheets and crayons or markers to students to work on while the facilitator reads the story, if desired.

Learning to Wait

Maurice always felt so wiggly. He just couldn't help himself. He struggled to sit still, wait for his turn, and stop himself from blurting. Every day, Ms. McDaniels called on him to get back in his seat, stop distracting his classmates, and stop yelling out.

Maurice wanted to wait patiently, but he didn't know how, and he felt like no matter how hard he tried, the wiggles always found their way out. Sometimes a thought would enter his head, and before he'd even realized what was happening, he was acting on that thought. Sometimes it was simple stuff like his pencil would need sharpening, or his water bottle would need to be filled, but sometimes the thoughts were more distracting, like rushing to the front of the line or hitting someone when they said something mean.

A couple of weeks ago, Ms. Henley, the school counselor, had asked to meet with Maurice. He hadn't wanted to go, but she'd said she had games, and even though he thought it might be a trick, he went with her. When he got there, he saw she wasn't kidding about the games. Her office was amazing!

Ms. Henley asked Maurice what he wanted to play with while he was there. He scanned the toys and found kinetic sand with rollers and cutters. She placed the bin in front of him, and he began to play. Ms. Henley had heard about what happened during gym class that day and asked Maurice about it. Maurice didn't want to share; it was so embarrassing. Ms. Henley tried again, "I heard you pushed someone out of your way while everyone was lined up. Could you tell me what happened?"

Maurice yelled, "It wasn't like that! Jeff cut in front of me, and I tried to move him back to his spot, but he fell. It was my turn!"

Ms. Henley nodded and said, "So, Jeff took your spot, and you moved him out of the way. Did I get that right?"

Maurice thought for a moment, "Yeah, I guess."

Ms. Henley nodded again, "Can I ask you a question?" Maurice shrugged, and Ms. Henley continued, "When you moved Jeff, did you mean to hurt him?"

Maurice looked surprised, "No! Never!"

And then Ms. Henley said, "Is it ever okay for us to touch other people out of frustration or without their permission?"

Maurice said softly, "No, it's not, but he was in my way, and I just couldn't wait."

Ms. Henley asked, "Is waiting something you struggle with?"

Maurice sighed, relieved to feel understood. "Yeah, it's hard for me to wait," he said.

Ms. Henley smiled. "Hey, that's okay. It's hard for most people to wait. It just takes practice."

Maurice was skeptical, "How do you practice waiting?"

Ms. Henley shrugged, "It's pretty simple, actually, but it's not always easy. What do you do now when you have to wait at the grocery store or the doctor's office?"

Maurice shrugged and said, "Probably play on my mom's phone."

Ms. Henley nodded, "I thought that might be the case. Running errands or going to the doctor are great opportunities to practice waiting without distracting yourself."

Maurice scrunched his face, "You want me to sit there and do nothing? That's so boring!"

Ms. Henley smiled, "When you sit still and notice the world around you, you learn to be patient. We could practice right now. Would that be okay?"

Maurice was hesitant, "I guess."

Ms. Henley asked him to put down the sand and sit with her. She said, "We're going to just sit here, and I want you to take in a few deep breaths and then see what you notice. I want you to notice any sounds you hear, pay attention to smells, the feel of the chair against your back, and then notice anything you see—sometimes you can pick a specific color and see how many places you notice it."

As he sat there, Maurice noticed the clock ticking, the smell of the food from the cafeteria, and the way his chair had gotten warmer as he sat there. When she was finished guiding him through noticing, Maurice looked up in surprise, "How'd you do that?"

"Do what?" Ms. Henley asked. "I hadn't noticed any of that stuff before you said something," Maurice replied.

Ms. Henley's face cracked into a big grin. "Exactly, because you were distracted. Once you notice how you feel and pay attention to your breath and your body, it is easier to notice when you're feeling impatient."

Maurice smiled, "That was pretty cool."

Ms. Henley agreed, "It's simple to practice paying attention, but it won't always be easy. It's one of those things that takes a lot of practice before you get good at it. Would you like some help practicing?"

Maurice nodded, "I'd like that."

DISCUSSION QUESTIONS

- How do you think Maurice might have felt before he pushed Jeff out of the way? What about after he pushed him?
- Do you think Maurice wants to be more patient? Is there evidence from the story to support your opinion?
- What were some strategies Ms. Henley suggested to practice being patient?
- What advice would you give Maurice to help him be more patient based on strategies you've used?

SKILL PRACTICE

Using the round-robin method, go around the table and ask students how they would practice each skill, giving each student a chance to answer one question. Skill practice can be adapted to allow students to answer in pairs or write their answers on scratch paper.

How Would You Practice Kindness If:

- You have to wait for your younger sister to finish playing with your iPad before you can have it?
- Your older brother is late picking you up and you have been waiting a long time?
- You are three dollars short of being able to buy your favorite toy?
- You're not allowed to get a dog until you're sixteen years old?
- You cannot go ice skating until your caregiver gets home from work?
- You want to make something to eat, but your caregiver is cleaning the kitchen floor?
- You are at the library with your family, but you would rather be playing soccer?
- Your friends want to play something different than what you want to play?
- You are the last one in line to get a piece of birthday cake?
- Your caregiver gets sick and cancels your camping weekend?

ADDITIONAL ACTIVITIES

- Conduct partner interviews. Ask students how they practice patience at school and in their home environments. Afterward, encourage each participant to share the patience-related skills their partner discussed with the entire group.
- We improve our patience when we become aware of our bodies and our surroundings. Take a color walk together as a group. Ask the group to choose a color and then go for a walk to find that color. While walking, be sure to notice your breath and each step you take. Try to stay quiet while walking and pay attention to all of your senses—what you see, hear, smell, feel, and taste. Adaptation: If you cannot take the group for a walk, ask them to complete the activity while sitting.

CLOSING CONSIDERATIONS

Patience means that we must have self-control and wait for things when we want them right away. It often means that we must use strategies to calm ourselves like breathing or reminding ourselves of our long-term goals.

Ask students to summarize the content of this session's lesson into a single sentence. Students will then consider how they will practice patience throughout the week. In pairs or groups of three, students may share their answers. If time allows, a few students may share with the whole group.

"WOULD YOU RATHER?" GAME

Playing the "Would You Rather?" game is a fun and engaging activity for students to develop their critical thinking skills. Students will reflect on their experience, evaluate their options based on their preferences, and reflect on the opinions of others, providing a different perspective and strengthening their sense of connection to one another.

WOULD YOU RATHER?

Copy and cut out the questions for small groups to discuss, or have each person stand in the center of the room and move towards one side or the other to show their vote for either option as the facilitator reads the questions aloud.

- WOULD YOU RATHER HAVE TO WAIT TO GO TO THE PARK OR PATIENTLY WAIT WITHOUT COMPLAINING?

- WOULD YOU RATHER WAIT QUIETLY OR EXPRESS YOUR FRUSTRATION TO LET THE PEOPLE MAKING YOU WAIT KNOW YOU'RE UPSET?

- WOULD YOU RATHER LISTEN TO A FRIEND'S STORY OR INTERRUPT THEM TO OFFER A SOLUTION TO THEIR PROBLEM?

- WOULD YOU RATHER SNEAK AND WATCH TV OR WAIT AND WATCH IT AFTER YOU'VE FINISHED YOUR HOMEWORK?

- WOULD YOU RATHER COMPLAIN THAT YOU WERE THE LAST ONE TO GET A TREAT IN YOUR CLASS OR SAY "THANK YOU" TO THE TEACHER PASSING IT OUT?

- WOULD YOU RATHER PLAY BY YOURSELF OR PLAY A GAME YOU DON'T LIKE WHILE WAITING FOR YOUR FRIENDS TO PLAY THE GAME YOU WANTED TO PLAY?

30-MINUTE GROUPS: LIFE SKILLS

> *Never give up on a dream just because of the time it will take to accomplish. The time will pass anyway.*
> EARL NIGHTINGALE

PATIENCE

30-MINUTE GROUPS: **LIFE SKILLS**

RESPECT

[*RESPECT: to feel or show honor or esteem for; to care for; show consideration for.*]

MIND MAP

On the board, draw a mind map and ask students to consider the meaning of *respect*.

ASCA® STANDARDS

- **B-SMS 1.** Responsibility for self and actions.
- **B-SS 8.** Advocacy skills for self and others and ability to assert self, when necessary.

DIRECTIONS

In a small group format, complete a brief check-in with your students by asking them to share a highlight and lowlight for the week or check in using the weather to represent their emotions. In a large group format, you might ask for a thumb up if they're feeling good, a thumb in the middle if they're feeling okay, and a thumb down if they aren't doing well. Review the Group Expectations before asking students to share their knowledge of the topic from the previous week. Together, review the Mind Map. Then, read the Lesson Introduction and ask the Circle Time Questions before reading the Story and asking the Discussion Questions. Students can work in pairs to craft their responses or share with the whole group. Complete the Skill Practice, "Would You Rather?" game, and Additional Activities as time allows. Be sure to complete the Closing Considerations with each lesson.

LESSON INTRODUCTION

Respect means treating others with thoughtfulness and care, and self-respect means caring about yourself and treating yourself with kindness and consideration. When we respect ourselves and others, we recognize the value in all human beings—strangers, friends, and ourselves and act in ways that are true to our identity. Without self-respect, we might let others take advantage of us and not care how others treat us. We show respect to others by listening, being polite, and taking care of others' belongings.

CIRCLE TIME QUESTIONS

Ask students to reflect and share their answers to the following questions with the group. Larger groups may need to be broken into smaller groups to give students ample time to share their answers and deepen the conversation.

- What situations make you feel most upset when someone isn't respectful to you?
- What are some ways that being impatient might make it seem like you aren't being respectful?
- What might happen if you aren't respectful to your classmates or teachers?

STORY TIME

Hand out coloring sheets and crayons or markers to students to work on while the facilitator reads the story, if desired.

Zoo Manners

Ms. Keith assigned Wes and Ben as field trip buddies for their Zoo adventure. Wes and Ben weren't exactly friends, but they usually got along okay if Wes did whatever Ben asked.

Wes liked Ben, but he was often unpredictable. Typically, when the boys played together, Ben insisted on playing games where he was the boss and made Wes work for him or threatened to kick him out of the game.

On the day of the field trip, Wes stood with his nose up to the glass, intently watching the tigers pace back and forth. Ben leaned close to his ear and said, "You should bang on the glass to get their attention." Wes stood perfectly still. He wasn't sure what to do. He didn't want to bother the tigers, but he was afraid of what Ben might do if he didn't comply.

Wes thought back to a conversation with his mother last week when he'd shared that at school that day, Ben had kicked him out of the game they were playing. Ben had gotten mad when Wes hadn't put mud on the teacher's bench as Ben had said to do. Wes' mom said, "Friends are kind, and they don't want to hurt your feelings or make you do things that make you uncomfortable or would get you in trouble. Other people may tell you that you have to do something, but it's up to you to respect yourself and decide what's right for you."

As the tigers paced, Wes turned to Ben and said, "No. I'm not doing that." Ben looked shocked and said, "Fine, be a baby," then banged on the glass and yelled for the tigers to "Do something cool!" Ms. Keith rushed to the boys and told Ben he'd need to be in her group now, and then she reassigned Wes to partner with Matt and Jake for the remainder of the field trip.

DISCUSSION QUESTIONS

- Why was Wes unsure of what to do when Ben told him to hit the glass?
- What might have happened if Wes had done what Ben had asked?
- What advice did Wes' mom give him about friendship and respect?
- How did Wes practice self-respect?

SKILL PRACTICE

Using the round-robin method, go around the table and ask students how they would practice each skill, giving every student a chance to answer one question. Skill practice can be adapted to allow students to answer in pairs or write their answers on scratch paper.

How Would You Practice Respect If:

- Your grandpa wants to give you advice on how to succeed in school?
- You borrowed a friend's bike?
- A teacher has given you an unexpected low grade on your science project?
- Your caregiver is on the phone and you want to ask them a question?
- You see a woman on crutches trying to open a door?
- Your coach chooses another soccer player to put in the game and you feel you're a better player?
- An elderly man spills his bag of groceries in front of you?
- Your friend is talking loudly to you in the library?
- A crossing guard asks you to get off your bike and walk it across a busy intersection?
- You work really hard on an essay and your teacher asks you to change three paragraphs?

ADDITIONAL ACTIVITIES

- In pairs, ask students to take turns being listeners and speakers. The speaker will share what has happened during their day. As they do, the listener will pretend to be respectful and disrespectful. The listener will be disrespectful by pretending to fidget, look away, and seem disinterested while the other person is talking. Then they will be respectful listeners; they nod along, lean forward, and make eye contact. The speaker will give a thumb up when the listener is pretending to be respectful and a thumb down when the speaker is pretending to be disrespectful. Each student should have the chance to play both roles.

- Break students into groups of two or three and ask them to write down how they could practice respect at home or school. Write "Respect at Home" and "Respect in School" on the board. Write down students' comments on the board and discuss the results of the activity. If a board is unavailable, ask students to share some of their results with the larger group and make a note of their responses on paper. Help students identify themes and expand upon their answers.

CLOSING CONSIDERATIONS

Respect helps us to get along with people. When we respect people, we consider their wants and needs and are open to listening and working together. Respect for someone lets us remember that we want to connect with the other person and see their side, even if we disagree. When we have self-respect, we have confidence in ourselves and want to act consistently with what is important to us.

Ask students to summarize the content of this session's lesson into a single sentence. Students will then consider how they will practice respect throughout the week. In pairs or groups of three, students may share their answers. If time allows, a few students may share with the whole group.

"WOULD YOU RATHER?" GAME

Playing the "Would You Rather?" game is a fun and engaging activity for students to develop their critical thinking skills. Students will reflect on their experience, evaluate their options based on their preferences, and reflect on the opinions of others, providing a different perspective and strengthening their sense of connection to one another.

WOULD YOU RATHER?

Copy and cut out the questions for small groups to discuss, or have each person stand in the center of the room and move towards one side or the other to show their vote for either option as the facilitator reads the questions aloud.

- WOULD YOU RATHER RETURN SOMETHING YOU BORROWED FROM A FRIEND THAT'S BROKEN OR ADMIT YOU BROKE IT AND APOLOGIZE?

- WOULD YOU RATHER TALK LOUDLY IN THE HALLWAY WITH YOUR FRIENDS OR BE QUIET SO YOU DON'T BOTHER THE STUDENTS IN THEIR CLASSROOMS?

- WOULD YOU RATHER FOLLOW THE FIRST REQUEST FROM YOUR TEACHER OR ARGUE?

- WOULD YOU RATHER SHOW RESPECT FOR YOUR COACH BY STAYING FOCUSED DURING PRACTICE OR GOOF OFF AND CHAT WITH FRIENDS?

- WOULD YOU RATHER SHOW RESPECT FOR YOUR CLASSMATES BY HELPING THEM WITH THEIR WORK OR LAUGH AT THEIR MISTAKES?

- WOULD YOU RATHER TALK WHILE YOUR TEACHER IS TALKING OR WAIT UNTIL THEY'RE FINISHED TO SAY WHAT YOU WANT TO SAY?

30-MINUTE GROUPS: **LIFE SKILLS**

GRATITUDE

[*GRATITUDE: being thankful for the big and little things, events, and people in our lives.*]

MIND MAP

On the board, draw a mind map and ask students to consider the meaning of *gratitude*.

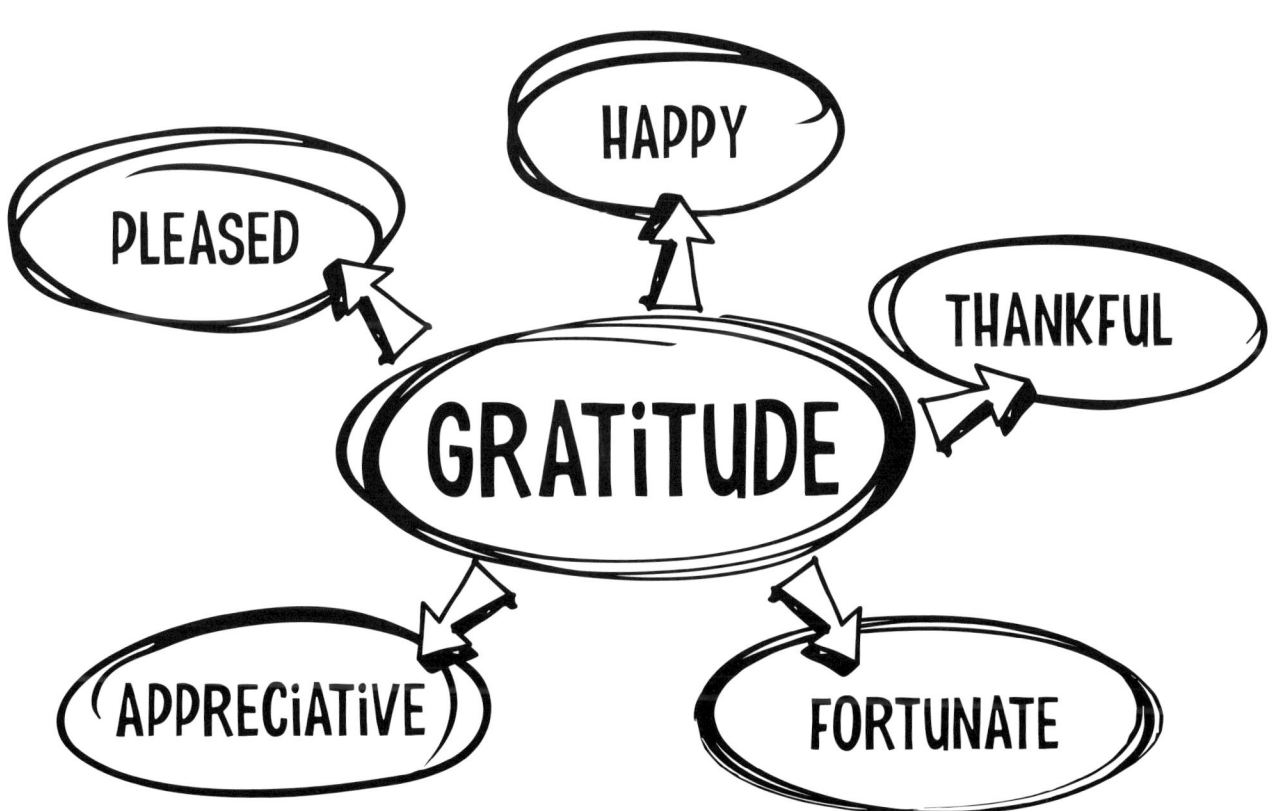

ASCA® STANDARDS

- **B-SS 2.** Positive, respectful, and supportive relationships with students who are similar to and different from them.
- **B-SS 9.** Social maturity and behaviors appropriate to the situation and environment.

DIRECTIONS

In a small group format, complete a brief check-in with your students by asking them to share a highlight and lowlight for the week or check in using the weather to represent their emotions. In a large group format, you might ask for a thumb up if they're feeling good, a thumb in the middle if they're feeling okay, and a thumb down if they aren't doing well. Review the Group Expectations before asking students to share their knowledge of the topic from the previous week. Together, review the Mind Map. Then, read the Lesson Introduction and ask the Circle Time Questions before reading the Story Time and asking the Discussion Questions. Students can work in pairs to craft their responses or share with the whole group. Complete the Skill Practice, "Would You Rather?" game, and Additional Activities as time allows. Be sure to complete the Closing Considerations with each lesson.

LESSON INTRODUCTION

Gratitude is feeling thankful and showing appreciation. When people are kind to us or give us things, we often feel grateful and want to return those feelings to them. We can show our feelings of gratitude by saying "thank you," writing "thank you" cards, or doing something nice for someone. There might be times when it can feel challenging to find anything to be grateful for and we might need to reach out to someone to help us find good things in our lives.

CIRCLE TIME QUESTIONS

Ask students to reflect and share their answers to the following questions with the group. Larger groups may need to be broken into smaller groups to give students ample time to share their answers and deepen the conversation.

- What is your favorite way to show gratitude to others?
- How do you feel when you practice gratitude?
- What might happen if you aren't grateful for the kindness others show?

STORY TIME

Hand out coloring sheets and crayons or markers to students to work on while the facilitator reads the story, if desired.

A Birthday Surprise!

Vanessa and Ming had been friends since they met last summer at Theater Camp. Since camp, they'd only played a few times together but always had so much fun when they hung out. So, when Vanessa invited Ming to her birthday party, she was so excited to see her again and couldn't wait to get her the perfect gift.

A few days before the party, Ming and her mom went to the store to pick out a gift for Vanessa. She considered different books, toys, and games for a long time before she finally settled on getting her a small silver necklace with a dog charm. Ming excitedly took the gift home, wrapped it in shiny paper, and put a colorful bow on top.

On the day of the party, Ming arrived, and Vanessa greeted her with a hug. All the kids played and ate cake, and then it was finally time to open gifts. Vanessa had a big plush chair in the center of the room, and all of the children and adults gathered around as she opened each gift one by one.

Soon, Vanessa picked up Ming's carefully wrapped gift and tore it open, revealing the necklace with a dog charm she'd bought. There was a pause, and then Vanessa's face scrunched up before she threw the chain down and said, "I don't like dogs!" The room was silent until Vanessa's mother walked over to pick up the necklace and quietly apologized to Ming. Ming looked on with tears as Vanessa continued to open more gifts.

DISCUSSION QUESTIONS

- What do you think Ming was feeling at the end of the story?
- Vanessa didn't like Ming's gift; how could she have avoided hurting Ming's feelings and still shown gratitude?
- How could Vanessa have expressed gratitude without lying about liking the gift?
- What do you think Vanessa might need to do if she wants to continue to be friends with Ming?

SKILL PRACTICE

Using the round-robin method, go around the table and ask students how they would practice each skill, giving every student a chance to answer one question. Skill practice can be adapted to allow students to answer in pairs or write their answers on scratch paper.

How Would You Practice Gratitude If:

- A family member is sick in the hospital?
- A neighbor brings over some freshly baked cookies to share with your family?
- Your teacher gives the class an extra fifteen minutes for recess?
- Your caregiver removes a stubborn stain from your favorite shirt?
- Your hands are full of groceries, and your younger sister holds the door open for you?
- You receive an invitation to a party from a classmate?
- A family member helps you with chores by hanging up your clean shirts?
- Someone compliments you for helping a teammate score a goal?
- An older family member helps you study for a spelling test?
- Someone pulls over and helps your caregiver change a flat tire?

ADDITIONAL ACTIVITIES

- Ask students to create a list of all the people, events, and things they appreciate in their lives. Remind students to be creative about things they might typically take for granted such as running water or access to education. Ask each student to share five things from their list with the group.

- Ask students to write a short "thank you" note to someone who has been kind to them recently. Have students be specific about what they are grateful for and how that kindness made them feel. Students can choose to share their notes with the recipient if they would like.

CLOSING CONSIDERATIONS

Gratitude is about being thankful and showing appreciation. Being grateful doesn't require us to lie if we receive a gift we don't like, but we can choose to share that information in a way that takes others' feelings into consideration.

Ask students to summarize the content of this session's lesson in a single sentence. Students will then consider how they will practice gratitude throughout the week. In pairs or groups of three, students may share their answers. If time allows, a few students may share with the group.

"WOULD YOU RATHER?" GAME

Playing the "Would You Rather?" game is a fun and engaging activity for students to develop their critical thinking skills. Students will reflect on their experience, evaluate their options based on their preferences, and reflect on the opinions of others, providing a different perspective and strengthening their sense of connection to one another.

WOULD YOU RATHER?

Copy and cut out the questions for small groups to discuss, or have each person stand in the center of the room and move towards one side or the other to show their vote for either option as the facilitator reads the questions aloud.

- WOULD YOU RATHER SAY "THANK YOU" FOR A GIFT YOU DON'T LIKE OR TELL THE GIVER YOU DON'T LIKE IT?

- WOULD YOU RATHER DO SOMETHING NICE FOR YOUR FRIEND WHO HELPED YOU OR WRITE A "THANK YOU" NOTE?

- WOULD YOU RATHER IGNORE SOMEONE WHO PICKED UP YOUR PENCIL OR SAY, "THANK YOU?"

- WOULD YOU RATHER SOMEONE THANK YOU FOR HOLDING THE DOOR OPEN FOR THEM OR BE IGNORED?

- WOULD YOU RATHER SOMEONE SAY "THANK YOU" FOR THE COOKIES YOU BROUGHT OR COMPLAIN THAT THEY AREN'T GOOD?

- WOULD YOU RATHER GIVE A GIFT TO SOMEONE WHO IS GRATEFUL OR SOMEONE WHO FEELS THEY DESERVE IT?

> *You cannot do a kindness too soon,
> for you never know how soon it will be too late.*
> RALPH WALDO EMERSON

GRATITUDE

RESPONSIBILITY

[*RESPONSIBILITY: sense of duty or obligation of taking care of someone or something; trustworthy; reliable; involving duties and obligations.*]

MIND MAP

On the board, draw a mind map and ask students to consider the meaning of *responsibility*.

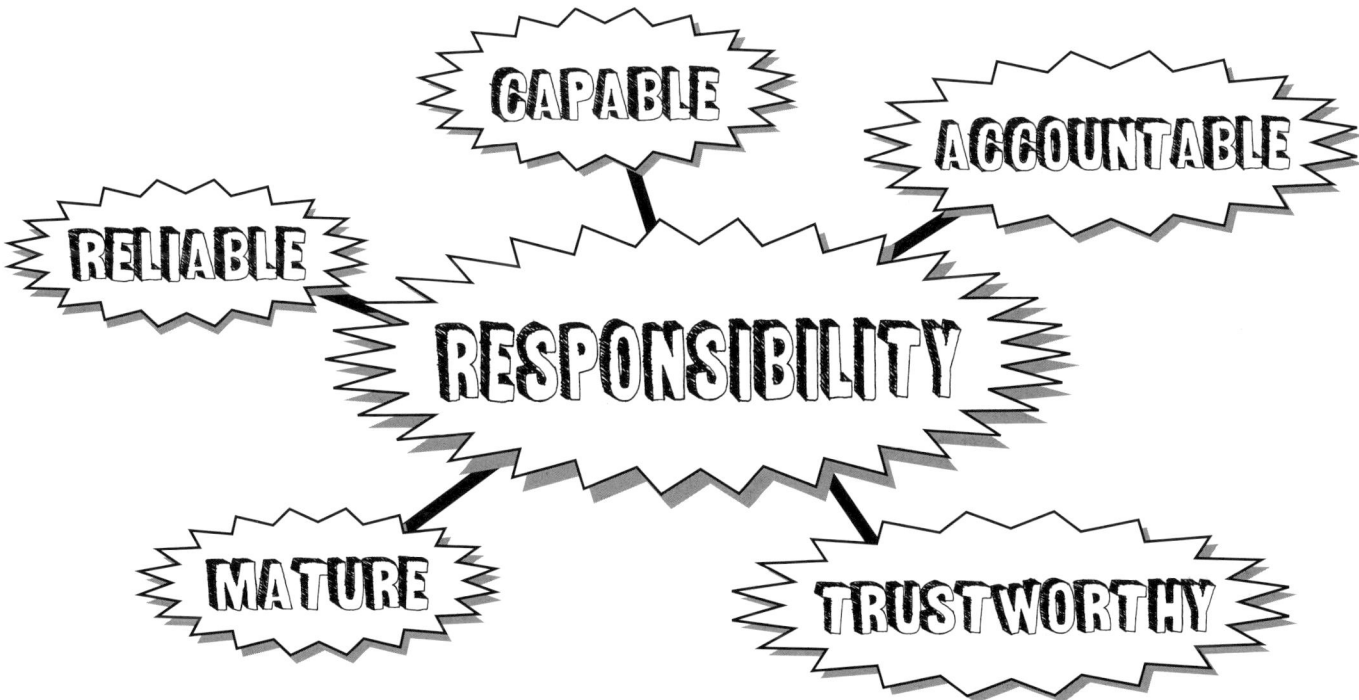

ASCA® STANDARDS

- **B-SMS 1.** Responsibility for self and actions.
- **B-SMS 2.** Self-discipline and self-control.
- **B-SMS 8.** Balance of school, home, and community activities.

DIRECTIONS

In a small group format, complete a brief check-in with your students by asking them to share a highlight and lowlight for the week or check in using the weather to represent their emotions. In a large group format, you might ask for a thumb up if they're feeling good, a thumb in the middle if they're feeling okay, and a thumb down if they aren't doing well. Review the Group Expectations before asking students to share their knowledge of the topic from the previous session. Together, review the Mind Map. Then, read the Lesson Introduction and ask the Circle Time Questions before reading the Story Time and asking the Discussion Questions. Students can work in pairs to craft their responses or share with the whole group. Complete the Skill Practice, "Would You Rather?" game, and Additional Activities as time allows. Be sure to complete the Closing Considerations with each lesson.

LESSON INTRODUCTION

Being responsible means that you can be trusted to do what you say you will do. Responsibility can include doing chores, turning in assignments, brushing your teeth, caring for belongings, or feeding your pet.

Responsible people do what is expected and keep their promises. Part of being responsible means we are reliable. It also means we don't over-commit and will ask for help when needed. Responsible people also admit when they have made a mistake and then work to fix the situation without blaming others or making excuses.

CIRCLE TIME QUESTIONS

Ask students to reflect and share their answers to the following questions with the group. Larger groups may need to be broken into smaller groups to give students ample time to share their answers and deepen the conversation.

- What are some ways you can act responsibly in your daily life?
- What are some consequences you might have if you choose not to behave responsibly?
- Why might we struggle to ask for help even when we know we need it?

STORY TIME

Hand out coloring sheets and crayons or markers to students to work on while the facilitator reads the story, if desired.

Taking Responsibility

Saha's family had put up a basketball goal over the garage, and she'd practiced all summer to get ready for tryouts. On the day of tryouts, all the girls were nervous while they waited for the call sheet to be listed on the outside of the gym door. Saha's stomach turned, wondering if she had worked hard enough to make the team. Was all her work about to pay off?

Finally, Coach B exited the gym and taped the list to the door. All the girls ran over to see if they'd made the list. Saha hung back, her nerves cementing her feet to the floor. When she finally got the courage to look, she saw her name on the list, "Saha Hensley, #17!" She'd done it! She made the team! Saha was thrilled and ready to start playing.

The basketball season was off to a great start. Saha was excellent, and even though she was only a high school freshman, the coach had put her in the starting lineup. Things were going well until the first grading reports came out.

Coach B took Saha aside and asked if she'd seen her grades. Saha hung her head. She had seen them, and they weren't good. Coach B reminded her that to play on the team, she'd need to keep at least a 'C' average.

Coach B praised Saha for being incredibly responsible at practice and working out without being reminded but told her that she needed to be accountable for her grades too. Saha nodded; she had wanted to do well but admitted that she'd gotten overwhelmed and didn't know what to do, so she'd tried to pretend everything was okay.

Coach B listened as Saha explained that she wasn't sure how to balance basketball, family time, friends, and school. She told him she'd been struggling in math and was often confused in class but wasn't sure what to do. "You can talk to me, Saha," Coach B said, "I can help set you up with a tutor. We are a team, and you are not alone, but you are responsible for communicating your needs. We can't help you if we don't know you need help."

Saha sighed. She knew Coach B was right, but she struggled to ask for help. Saha didn't always trust that grownups would do what they said they would do because her biological parents hadn't been reliable.

As she thought about it, she realized she didn't want to let the past ruin her present. Things were getting better now; Saha's adoptive family was reliable, and she was determined to be the kind of person that other people could count on. She paused and looked up at Coach B, "I'd be grateful to have a tutor. Thanks, Coach."

DISCUSSION QUESTIONS

- Sometimes, we can be responsible in one area of our life and not another. In what ways does Saha demonstrate responsibility in the story?
- How can we know that basketball was important to Saha?
- What consequences does Saha face if she fails to be responsible?
- What might have happened if Saha had blamed her poor grades on someone else?

SKILL PRACTICE

Using the round-robin method, go around the table and ask students how they would practice each skill, giving every student a chance to answer one question. Skill practice can be adapted to allow students to answer in pairs or write their answers on scratch paper.

How Would You Practice Responsibility If:

- You are on the final level of your favorite video game, and you remember that your science project is due tomorrow?
- You just broke a framed picture of your family because you were playing with a ball in the house?
- Your grandmother asks you to watch your younger brother while she goes outside to water the garden?
- You're watching a movie at a friend's house, and it is time for you to go home?
- You need to do your part in the group project, but you'd rather play kickball after school than go to the library?
- Your sister is not feeling well, and your caregiver asks you to take over her chores for the weekend?
- You borrowed your neighbor's rollerblades?
- Your friend asks you to play, but you promised your caregiver you would put away the clean dishes?
- Your coach asks you to come to practice on time, but you'd rather hang out with friends?
- Your caregiver asks you to clean your room before guests arrive?

ADDITIONAL ACTIVITIES

- Ask students to draw representations of them being responsible. Ask students to share their drawings with the group and explain the scene.
- Set a timer and ask students to list how they practice being responsible at home in three minutes. Pair students and ask them to review their list and look for similarities and differences with their partner. If time allows, ask each pair to share one of their similarities with the group.

CLOSING CONSIDERATIONS

Being responsible means taking ownership of your actions and being accountable for the consequences. Even when you make mistakes, like Saha, you take responsibility for your actions and don't make excuses or blame others. You also try to do whatever you can to make the situation better. When you demonstrate responsibility, people are more likely to trust you and give you more privileges and freedoms.

Ask students to summarize the content of this session's lesson into a single sentence. Students will then consider how they will practice responsibility throughout the week. In pairs or groups of three, students may share their answers. If time allows, a few students may share with the whole group.

"WOULD YOU RATHER?" GAME

Playing the "Would You Rather?" game is a fun and engaging activity for students to develop their critical thinking skills. Students will reflect on their experience, evaluate their options based on their preferences, and reflect on the opinions of others, providing a different perspective and strengthening their sense of connection to one another.

WOULD YOU RATHER?

Copy and cut out the questions for small groups to discuss, or have each person stand in the center of the room and move towards one side or the other to show their vote for either option as the facilitator reads the questions aloud.

- WOULD YOU RATHER TELL YOUR TEACHER YOU BROKE THE PENCIL SHARPENER OR PRETEND IT DIDN'T HAPPEN?

- WOULD YOU RATHER SET A REMINDER TO DO YOUR HOMEWORK OR HOPE YOU WON'T FORGET?

- WOULD YOU RATHER SET AN ALARM CLOCK TO WAKE YOURSELF UP ON SCHOOL DAYS OR ASK YOUR GROWNUP TO WAKE YOU?

- WOULD YOU RATHER HANG YOUR JACKET WHEN YOU GET HOME OR THROW IT ON THE FLOOR FOR SOMEONE ELSE TO PICK UP?

- WOULD YOU RATHER GIVE YOUR PET WATER WHEN THEY NEED IT OR WAIT TO BE TOLD?

- WOULD YOU RATHER GET YOURSELF READY FOR BED OR WAIT UNTIL YOUR GROWNUP TELLS YOU IT'S TIME?

Honesty

[*HONESTY: truthful and genuine; fair and upright; not lying, cheating, or stealing; obtained by fair means; not hiding one's real nature; frank and open.*]

MIND MAP

On the board, draw a mind map and ask students to consider the meaning of *honesty*.

30-MINUTE GROUPS: LIFE SKILLS

ASCA® STANDARDS

- **B-SS 2.** Positive, respectful, and supportive relationships with students who are similar to and different from them.
- **B-SS 5.** Ethical decision-making and social responsibility.
- **B-SMS** 1. Responsibility for self and actions.

DIRECTIONS

In a small group format, complete a brief check-in with your students by asking them to share a highlight and lowlight for the week or check in using the weather to represent their emotions. In a large group format, you might ask for a thumb up if they're feeling good, a thumb in the middle if they're feeling okay, and a thumb down if they aren't doing well. Review the Group Expectations before asking students to share their knowledge of the topic from the previous week. Together, review the Mind Map. Then, read the Lesson Introduction and ask the Circle Time Questions before reading the Story Time and asking the Discussion Questions. Students can work in pairs to craft their responses or share with the whole group. Complete the Skill Practice, "Would You Rather?" game, and Additional Activities as time allows. Be sure to complete the Closing Considerations with each lesson.

LESSON INTRODUCTION

Honesty is telling the truth, even when it's scary to do so. Sometimes it can be difficult to tell the truth because we are worried that we will get in trouble, someone will get mad, or we will suffer harsh consequences. Sometimes it feels easier to lie if we believe that lying might get us out of a tricky situation.

People who aren't honest often have to tell lots of lies to support their original lie. And when people discover that they've been lied to, their feelings may be hurt, and their belief that we will tell the truth in the future is gone. Being honest may not always be comfortable or get us what we want, but being truthful allows us to feel good about ourselves, regardless of the consequences we face.

A word of caution: While it's important for us to tell the truth, we should remember that we don't have to share the truth in a harsh or unkind way. Telling our best friend that they have something in their teeth in front of the whole lunch table might be helpful and true, but it wouldn't be kind. We can find ways to be honest without being hurtful.

CIRCLE TIME QUESTIONS

Ask students to reflect and share their answers to the following questions with the group. Larger groups may need to be broken into smaller groups to give students ample time to share their answers and deepen the conversation.

- What are the typical reasons that people might not be honest?
- Have you ever been afraid to be honest about a mistake you've made?
- What are some strategies we can use to be less reactive when someone is honest with us about something we don't want to hear?

STORY TIME

Hand out coloring sheets and crayons or markers to students to work on while the facilitator reads the story, if desired.

Finding the Truth in Grades

Brynn felt sick to her stomach; it felt like the time she was too scared to jump off the high dive at the pool last summer. However, she wasn't too high on the diving board. She was sitting on the bus with her classmates, trying to make the signature on her report card look like her mother's.

Brynn's hands were shaking, and her heart was racing. Everything felt wrong. But she kept practicing her mom's signature on a blank piece of notebook paper, trying to get the 'S' just right in her mom's curvy handwriting. She actually felt sick. She was having second thoughts. Maybe she should tell her parents about her grade, but the idea of disappointing them felt unbearable.

Brynn was confident she could get her grade up before the next report card, but she'd let things slide this semester. She needed to figure out where things went wrong. Maybe she'd spent a little too much time with her friends, or perhaps she was spending too much time playing video games. Either way, she'd messed up her math grade. Brynn loved math; it had always come so easily for her, so she thought she could get by without studying, but that didn't seem to be the case after all.

Now she would have to lie to get herself out of trouble. Was she really going to do this? Suddenly the bus jerked forward, and as she looked up, she caught the gaze of Jess, sitting across the aisle from her. Jess gave her a look, saying she knew what Brynn was up to. Her heart sank. Now she would be a liar, and someone would know about it. "Great, just great," she thought to herself. Jess motioned to ask if she could move to sit with Brynn. Brynn nodded 'yes,' not knowing what else to do, and Jess moved in next to her.

Jess pointed to Brynn's practice signatures and smiled, "Whatcha doin'?"

Brynn said, "You know what I'm doing."

Jess agreed, "I do. But can I ask why you're doing it?"

Brynn stared out the window for a long moment and said, "I don't want my parents to know I messed up."

Jess said, "I see. Will they be mad or yell at you?"

Brynn looked surprised, "No, they'll just be disappointed. They only ask that I try my best, but I didn't. I got distracted and thought I had things under control, but clearly, I didn't."

Jess shook her head, "Right, so you messed up, and now you know how to fix that mistake. But if you do this, you're lying. How will your parents feel about that?"

Brynn leaned her head against the seat in front of her. "Ugh, I hate that you're right. If I lie, they'll never trust me again, will they? You think I should just tell them, don't you?"

Jess shrugged, "Do whatever you think is best."

Brynn sighed loudly, "I'm nervous about telling them, but I really don't think I want to do this," as she waved her hand over the signatures on her notebook. She took a deep breath, "That's it. I'm just going to tell them. If I get caught forging my mom's signature, then it's going to be even worse. So, whatever happens will happen, but I don't want to be the kind of person that lies."

DISCUSSION QUESTIONS

- Why do you think Brynn's heart was racing and she felt sick? What might her body have been trying to tell her?
- Why do you think Brynn was nervous about sharing her report card with her parents?
- What might happen if Brynn was caught lying about her grade?

SKILL PRACTICE

Using the round-robin method, go around the table and ask students how they would practice each skill, giving every student a chance to answer one question. Skill practice can be adapted to allow students to answer in pairs or write their answers on scratch paper.

How Would You Practice Honesty If:

- Your friend gives you a gift you don't like?
- You tell your best friend's secret to another friend and your best friend finds out?
- You forget to clean your room and your caregiver asks again if it is clean?
- Your friend asks if her new glasses look good on her, but you don't think they do?
- You exaggerate to your friends about how well you did in your soccer game?
- Your friends want you to take some candy from the store?
- Your teacher wants to know where your project is, but you haven't finished it?
- A classmate, who you do not like, wants to borrow a piece of paper?
- Your caregiver wants to know if you have finished your homework. At the same time, your friends want you to come outside and play.
- Your caregiver tells you to stop playing on your computer, but you know they won't find out if you keep playing.

ADDITIONAL ACTIVITIES

- Ask students to write a short journal entry that describes a time when they were being honest. It may have been when they had to tell a caregiver or friend the truth. The journal entry should include how they felt before and after they practiced honesty.

- Ask students to draw a picture of a time when they practiced being honest. Have them explain the picture to the group.

CLOSING CONSIDERATIONS

Honesty means that we tell the truth even if we might not like the consequences. Honesty and trust are the foundation of all good relationships.

Ask students to summarize the content of this session's lesson into a single sentence. Students will then consider how they will practice honesty throughout the week. In pairs or groups of three, students may share their answers. If time allows, a few students may share with the whole group.

"WOULD YOU RATHER?" GAME

Playing the "Would You Rather?" game is a fun and engaging activity for students to develop their critical thinking skills. Students will reflect on their experience, evaluate their options based on their preferences, and reflect on the opinions of others, providing a different perspective and strengthening their sense of connection to one another.

Would You Rather?

Copy and cut out the questions for small groups to discuss, or have each person stand in the center of the room and move towards one side or the other to show their vote for either option as the facilitator reads the questions aloud.

- WOULD YOU RATHER TELL THE TRUTH, EVEN IF IT HURTS SOMEONE'S FEELINGS OR LIE TO KEEP FROM HURTING SOMEONE'S FEELINGS?

- WOULD YOU RATHER BE HONEST, EVEN IF IT GETS YOU INTO TROUBLE OR LIE TO GET OUT OF TROUBLE?

- WOULD YOU RATHER ADMIT WHEN YOU DON'T KNOW SOMETHING OR PRETEND TO KNOW SOMETHING YOU DON'T?

- WOULD YOU RATHER KEEP YOUR PROMISE AND NOT SHARE A SECRET OR PRETEND YOU DIDN'T SHARE SOMEONE'S SECRET?

- WOULD YOU RATHER PRETEND YOU DID BETTER ON A TEST THAN YOU ACTUALLY DID OR TELL THE TRUTH THAT YOU DIDN'T DO WELL?

- WOULD YOU RATHER KEEP A COOL TOY THAT YOU FOUND IN THE HALLWAY OR RETURN IT TO THE LOST AND FOUND?

30-MINUTE GROUPS: LIFE SKILLS

CHAPTER 7

Friendship

[*FRIENDSHIP: having a close personal companion; having mutual respect for someone.*]

MIND MAP

On the board, draw a mind map and ask students to consider the meaning of *friendship*.

- COMRADE
- SUPPORTER
- FRIENDSHIP
- ALLY
- ADVOCATE

30-MINUTE GROUPS: LIFE SKILLS

ASCA® STANDARDS

- **B-SS 1.** Effective oral and written communication skills and listening skills.
- **B-SS 2.** Positive, respectful, and supportive relationships with students who are similar to and different from them.
- **B-SMS 7.** Effective coping skills.

DIRECTIONS

In a small group format, complete a brief check-in with your students by asking them to share a highlight and lowlight for the week or check in using the weather to represent their emotions. In a large group format, you might ask for a thumb up if they're feeling good, a thumb in the middle if they're feeling okay, and a thumb down if they aren't doing well. Review the Group Expectations before asking students to share their knowledge of the topic from the previous week. Together, review the Mind Map. Then, read the Lesson Introduction and ask the Circle Time Questions before reading the Story Time and asking the Discussion Questions. Students can work in pairs to craft their responses or share with the whole group. Complete the Skill Practice, "Would You Rather?" game, and Additional Activities as time allows. Be sure to complete the Closing Considerations with each lesson.

LESSON INTRODUCTION

Friendship is when people like each other and want to spend time together. Friends can look different and have different interests, but they have in common that they want what is best for the other person and care about their well-being. We can have more than one friend. Sometimes, we have friends we see at school but don't see outside of school; some friends we might talk to daily, and some we don't see as often. Good friends don't threaten to take away their friendship if we spend time with other people or do activities they aren't interested in. Friends can trust that the other person has their best interest in mind and will be honest with them. We don't have to worry that our friends will share our secrets or make fun of us because we know they care about us and don't want to hurt us.

CIRCLE TIME QUESTIONS

Ask students to reflect and share their answers to the following questions with the group. Larger groups may need to be broken into smaller groups to give students ample time to share their answers and deepen the conversation.

- What are some qualities of a good friend?
- What might be some warning signs that a friend is not kind or safe?
- Who might you talk to if you found yourself in an unsafe situation with a friend?

STORY TIME

Hand out coloring sheets and crayons or markers to students to work on while the facilitator reads the story, if desired.

The Magic Formula for Friendship

Alex and Hooman met when Alex moved into the house next door. The two were nearly inseparable and often used the gap in the fence to go to each other's homes. On Fridays, Alex's mom would order a pizza, and they'd eat in Hooman's treehouse and watch goofy comedies on his laptop.

Or at least they did up until last Friday. Alex was supposed to come over like he always did for pizza and movies, but he never showed. When Hooman texted him to see where he was, he said, "Sorry, I forgot. I'm having dinner with the team." Not only had he forgotten their tradition, but he'd also forgotten to tell Hooman he wasn't coming. Hooman knew Alex was busier now that he'd joined the soccer team, but he hadn't thought he would forget about their friendship so quickly.

When Alex texted Hooman that weekend to hang out, Hooman ignored him. At school on Monday, Alex tried to talk to Hooman, but he pretended he didn't hear him and walked away.

Finally, on Monday night, Alex pushed through the broken fence and climbed the ladder to the treehouse, where he found Hooman. "Please talk to me," Alex pleaded. Hooman gave him an icy stare; he was so angry. Then he decided he'd try to fix their friendship rather than be angry. Hooman used the "magic formula" he'd learned in class to express his emotions. He remembered three parts; how you felt, what happened, and what you'd need to move forward. ("I feel ____ when ____. Please ____.")

With a shaky breath, he said, "I felt betrayed and disappointed when you canceled on me without even telling me. Please don't leave me hanging like that again."

Alex looked at his shoes; he knew he'd messed up and would have to admit it if he wanted forgiveness. Alex sucked in a breath and said, "You're right. I'm sorry. I was so excited to have been invited out with the team and I forgot to tell you. I should've reached out. It won't happen again. Will you forgive me?" Hooman's face softened, and he agreed to give their friendship another chance.

DISCUSSION QUESTIONS

- Why do you think Hooman avoided talking to Alex?
- What is the "magic formula" that Hooman and Alex used to communicate during their conflict?
- How did Hooman and Alex each show courage and bravery?
- What might have happened if Alex hadn't taken responsibility and apologized to Hooman?

SKILL PRACTICE

Using the round-robin method, go around the table and ask students how they would practice each skill, giving every student a chance to answer one question. Skill practice can be adapted to allow students to answer in pairs or write their answers on scratch paper.

How Would You Practice Friendship If:

- Your friend doesn't want to play the same game that you want to play?
- You forget your friend's birthday?
- Your best friend wants to play with someone else?
- You heard a rumor that someone was saying mean things about your friend?
- Your friend is already sitting with other people when you get to the cafeteria?
- Your friend plays on the other sports team and they beat your team?
- Your friend asks you for a piece of gum and you only have one more?
- You and your best friend like the same sweater at the store, but there is only one left.
- You study so hard for the test and your friend doesn't study at all, but they get a better grade?
- You are staying the night with your friend, and they want to go to another friend's house. But you only have permission to be at their house.

ADDITIONAL ACTIVITIES

- Pair students and ask them to resolve this conflict by practicing using the magic formula. Scenario: Your friend was supposed to message you over the weekend, and they didn't. Use the magic formula, "I feel _____ when _____. Please _____." Ask students to share how they resolved the conflict with the group.

- Ask students to draw four circles, one inside the other. Encourage them to place themselves in the center, then list the people closest to them inside the smallest circle and those less close to them in the outer circles. For example, your best friend will go in the circle closest to you, but a cousin you rarely see might go in one of the outer rings. Then pair students and ask them to make a list of the friendship qualities of the people in their closest circles. Ask the pairs to share the good friendship qualities with the group and look for overlap between groups.

CLOSING CONSIDERATIONS

Friends care about one another and want what is best for them, but sometimes they hurt each other's feelings and need to make amends.

Ask students to summarize the content of this session's lesson into a single sentence. Students will then consider how they will practice being a good friend throughout the week. In pairs or groups of three, students may share their answers. If time allows, a few students may share with the whole group.

"WOULD YOU RATHER?" GAME

Playing the "Would You Rather?" game is a fun and engaging activity for students to develop their critical thinking skills. Students will reflect on their experience, evaluate their options based on their preferences, and reflect on the opinions of others, providing a different perspective and strengthening their sense of connection to one another.

Would You Rather?

Copy and cut out the questions for small groups to discuss, or have each person stand in the center of the room and move towards one side or the other to show their vote for either option as the facilitator reads the questions aloud.

WOULD YOU RATHER HAVE ONE CLOSE FRIEND OR MANY PEOPLE YOU DON'T KNOW THAT WELL?

WOULD YOU RATHER HAVE A FRIEND WHO'S SUPER OUTGOING OR A FRIEND WHO PREFERS QUIET ACTIVITIES?

WOULD YOU RATHER HAVE A FRIEND WHO ALWAYS AGREES WITH YOU OR A FRIEND WHO CHALLENGES YOU WHEN YOU'RE WRONG?

WOULD YOU RATHER HAVE A FRIEND WHO SHARES ALL YOUR INTERESTS AND HOBBIES OR SOMEONE WHO DOESN'T LIKE THE SAME THINGS YOU LIKE?

WOULD YOU RATHER HAVE A FRIEND WHO'S WILLING TO APOLOGIZE WHEN THEY HURT YOUR FEELINGS OR A FRIEND WHO REFUSES TO APOLOGIZE?

WOULD YOU RATHER HAVE A FRIEND WHO HAS OTHER FRIENDS OR SOMEONE WHO ONLY EVER WANTS TO SPEND TIME WITH YOU?

30-MINUTE GROUPS: LIFE SKILLS

Compassion

[*COMPASSION: being aware of others' troubles and wanting to help; empathy.*]

MIND MAP

On the board, draw a mind map and ask students to consider the meaning of *compassion*.

ASCA® STANDARDS:

- **B-SS 4.** Empathy.
- **B-SS 5.** Ethical decision-making and social responsibility.
- **B-SS 6.** Effective collaboration and cooperation skills.

DIRECTIONS

In a small group format, complete a brief check-in with your students by asking them to share a highlight and lowlight for the week or check in using the weather to represent their emotions. In a large group format, you might ask for a thumb up if they're feeling good, a thumb in the middle if they're feeling okay, and a thumb down if they aren't doing well. Review the Group Expectations before asking students to share their knowledge of the topic from the previous week. Together, review the Mind Map. Then, read the Lesson Introduction and ask the Circle Time Questions before reading the Story Time and asking the Discussion Questions. Students can work in pairs to craft their responses or share with the whole group. Complete the Skill Practice, "Would You Rather?" game, and Additional Activities as time allows. Be sure to complete the Closing Considerations with each lesson.

LESSON INTRODUCTION

Compassion is when you have concern for the feelings of others. We can't feel someone else's pain, but a compassionate person tries to understand why a person is experiencing pain, whether it is physical or emotional. Have you ever watched a video of someone falling? Did it make you hurt for them? That's empathy. And if you wanted to help them, that's compassion.

You can imagine feeling someone else's pain, even if you don't know that person or have never had their experience. Compassion means that you can imagine what it's like to experience what they're experiencing. Rather than responding reflexively, we can imagine the situation through the other person's eyes and consider what they might be feeling.

You can practice compassion by forgiving someone who accidentally hurts you, encouraging someone who does poorly on a test, or helping a new student feel accepted. Compassion is about imagining yourself in their experience and then treating them how you'd want to be treated.

CIRCLE TIME QUESTIONS

Ask students to reflect and share their answers to the following questions with the group. Larger groups may need to be broken into smaller groups to give students ample time to share their answers and deepen the conversation.

- What might you say to encourage your friend if they are going through a hard time?
- We can feel angry at ourselves when we make a mistake and speak to ourselves unkindly. What might we say to show compassion to ourselves? (Hint: Imagine what you might say to a friend.)
- Consider what causes you pain. How can you act in a way that would ensure you won't cause that pain for others? (Example: Being left out can be painful, so you might make sure to include everyone.)

STORY TIME

Hand out coloring sheets and crayons or markers to students to work on while the facilitator reads the story, if desired.

The Power of Compassion

Malik, Genevieve, Elliot, and Landon were grouped together for the upcoming solar system project. The group was loud and rambunctious. Everyone except Malik. Malik was shy and typically liked to keep to himself, but he was incredible at science and loved talking about the solar system.

One day during class, the groups were allowed to scatter in the field behind the school to work on their project together. They were all so excited to be outside in the warm weather that they were even louder than usual, and when they sat down, they all started talking at the same time. Genevieve noticed that each time Malik would begin to speak, the other boys would talk over him, and eventually he just stopped talking. Genevieve could imagine how frustrated Malik must feel when he was constantly interrupted and talked over. She knew it wasn't his style to raise his voice, so she spoke for him even though she was uncomfortable standing up to Elliot and Landon.

Genevieve stopped the other boys from talking and directed the conversation back to Malik by saying, "Hey guys, it looks like Malik has an idea. Let's listen to him. He knows lots about the solar system." Malik looked surprised and smiled at Genevieve, and then quietly began to share his ideas with the group. Everyone listened, and they were shocked. Malik knew so much more about the topic than they could have imagined, and his ideas for their project were going to really help them stand out.

DISCUSSION QUESTIONS

- What might Malik have been feeling when the group was ignoring him?
- How did Genevieve show compassion to Malik?
- How might Genevieve's gesture of kindness have made Malik feel?
- What might have happened if Genevieve hadn't spoken up for Malik?

SKILL PRACTICE

Using the round-robin method, go around the table and ask students how they would practice each skill, giving every student a chance to answer one question. Skill practice can be adapted to allow students to answer in pairs or write their answers on scratch paper.

How Would You Practice Compassion If:

- You see a friend fall down while playing outside?
- You have one piece of candy left in your pocket and you'd like to eat it, but you're playing at the park with several friends?

- The neighbor's cat has a thorn stuck in its paw?
- Your younger brother ends up in last place during his swim event?
- Your sister is crying because she lost the ten dollars Grandma gave her for her birthday?
- You've been asked to write down the homework assignment for a sick classmate?
- A quiet student is eating lunch alone near you in the cafeteria?
- Your best friend is sad because he didn't get picked for the basketball team?
- Someone you don't like accidentally bumps into your desk and knocks over all of your papers?
- A classmate is sad because his caregiver is in the hospital?

ADDITIONAL ACTIVITIES

- Practice empathetic listening with this exercise. Break the group into pairs and assign a listener and a speaker. Ask the speaker to share a story about their favorite day with the listener. The listener is to repeat the story back to them as they heard it and then try to guess how the speaker was feeling during their favorite day. Switch roles so that all students have the chance to practice both roles.
- Ask students to think of someone special, and then, if they are comfortable, ask them to close their eyes and imagine sending well wishes and good thoughts to that person for one minute. When the activity is complete, ask the students to share their experiences with the group.

CLOSING CONSIDERATIONS

Compassion is being thoughtful about the experiences of others and imagining how they are seeing the world; with a desire to help them or better their situation.

Ask students to summarize the content of this session's lesson into a single sentence. Students will then consider how they will practice compassion throughout the week. In pairs or groups of three, students may share their answers. If time allows, a few students may share with the whole group.

"WOULD YOU RATHER?" GAME

Playing the "Would You Rather?" game is a fun and engaging activity for students to develop their critical thinking skills. Students will reflect on their experience, evaluate their options based on their preferences, and reflect on the opinions of others, providing a different perspective and strengthening their sense of connection to one another.

Would You Rather?

Copy and cut out the questions for small groups to discuss, or have each person stand in the center of the room and move towards one side or the other to show their vote for either option as the facilitator reads the questions aloud.

- WOULD YOU RATHER SIT WITH YOUR CLASSMATE WHO IS ALONE AT LUNCH OR LEAVE THEM TO EAT ALONE?

- WOULD YOU RATHER LISTEN TO YOUR FRIEND AS THEY TELL YOU ABOUT THEIR BAD DAY OR INTERRUPT TO TELL ABOUT YOUR BAD DAY?

- WOULD YOU RATHER HELP A CLASSMATE WHO IS BEING BULLIED OR JOIN IN AND MAKE FUN OF THEM?

- WOULD YOU RATHER YELL AT YOUR CLASSMATE FOR STEPPING ON YOUR SHOES OR ACCEPT THEIR APOLOGY?

- WOULD YOU RATHER SIGN A GET-WELL CARD FOR YOUR SICK TEACHER OR SKIP IT BECAUSE OTHER PEOPLE WILL SIGN IT?

- WOULD YOU RATHER GIVE A COMPLIMENT TO A CLASSMATE WHO LOOKS SAD OR IGNORE THEM?

30-MINUTE GROUPS: **LIFE SKILLS**

FORGIVENESS

[*FORGIVENESS: the act of forgiving; pardon; overlook; let go; excuse or absolve; to stop blaming or feeling resentment against.*]

MIND MAP

On the board, draw a mind map and ask students to consider the meaning of *forgiveness*.

30-MINUTE GROUPS: LIFE SKILLS

ASCA® STANDARDS

- **B-SS 2.** Positive, respectful, and supportive relationships with students who are similar to and different from them.
- **B-SS 4.** Empathy.
- **B-SS 5.** Ethical decision-making and social responsibility.

DIRECTIONS

In a small group format, complete a brief check-in with your students by asking them to share a highlight and lowlight for the week or check in using the weather to represent their emotions. In a large group format, you might ask for a thumb up if they're feeling good, a thumb in the middle if they're feeling okay, and a thumb down if they aren't doing well. Review the Group Expectations before asking students to share their knowledge of the topic from the previous week. Together, review the Mind Map. Then, read the Lesson Introduction and ask the Circle Time Questions before reading the Story Time and asking the Discussion Questions. Students can work in pairs to craft their responses or share with the whole group. Complete the Skill Practice, "Would You Rather?" game, and Additional Activities as time allows. Be sure to complete the Closing Considerations with each lesson. Remind students that the group will soon be coming to a close.

LESSON INTRODUCTION

Everyone makes mistakes—it's part of being human. Forgiveness means giving someone another chance, even when we may feel hurt or disappointed. When we offer forgiveness, we create a second chance for that relationship to heal.

Sometimes we might make mistakes with our friends by saying something wrong or acting in a way that hurts someone's feelings. When that happens, we need to apologize and ask for forgiveness. We also have to agree to try to avoid making that mistake again. It can be frustrating to make mistakes and we may want to punish ourselves for messing up, but we also need to forgive ourselves. Forgiving yourself means you stop blaming and punishing yourself and make an effort to do better in the future. Mistakes are how we learn and grow.

CIRCLE TIME QUESTIONS

Ask students to reflect and share their answers to the following questions with the group. Larger groups may need to be broken into smaller groups to give students ample time to share their answers and deepen the conversation.

- Has there been a time when you have been forgiven but didn't feel like you deserved it?
- What might you say to forgive yourself after you've made a mistake?
- When might someone not deserve your forgiveness?

STORY TIME

Hand out coloring sheets and crayons or markers to students to work on while the facilitator reads the story, if desired.

The Secret Keeper

Amalie knew she'd shared too much almost as soon as the words left her lips. Amalie was talking to her friend Katie. Katie shared that her parents were separating, and she wasn't sure how she should feel about the situation. Without thinking, Amalie said, "You should talk to Marcella; her parents are getting a divorce. Maybe you can ask her what that's like."

Marcella's parents splitting up was a secret that Amalie wasn't supposed to share. Marcella and Amalie were neighbors and had been friends since kindergarten. They shared everything and trusted each other to keep their secrets. Amalie felt guilt and fear because she knew she'd shared a secret she shouldn't have shared. She didn't know what to do and felt sick about the situation.

When Amalie's mom came to pick her up from school, Amalie threw her bag in the backseat, and as she climbed in, said, "Mom, I think I messed up. I accidentally shared a secret I wasn't supposed to share." Amalie's mom listened to what had happened, and then asked, "What do you think you need to do about this situation to make it right?" Amalie sighed, "I have to tell Marcella I shared her secret, don't I?" Her mom smiled in the rearview mirror and said, "What happens if you don't tell her and someone else does?" Amalie knew that would be worse than telling Marcella what she'd done.

Amalie went to Marcella's house and rang the doorbell as soon as she got home. Marcella answered the door, and Amalie immediately launched into an apology. She said, "Marcella, I'm so sorry. I talked with Katie today and accidentally shared that your parents were separating. I know that wasn't my secret to share. I'm so sorry."

Marcella looked stunned and asked, "Why would you do that?" Amalie looked down at her shoes, unsure what to say because she didn't want to share Katie's secret without permission. Instead, she said, "Katie is going through some things at home, and I thought she might be able to talk to you about it."

Marcella's face softened, and she said, "That makes sense. So, you didn't mean to share my business?" Amalie rushed to speak, "No, never. I just didn't think before I spoke. Will you forgive me?" Marcella took a long breath before saying, "I'll forgive you, but please be thoughtful with my secrets in the future." Amalie agreed, and the girls headed off to play outside.

DISCUSSION QUESTIONS

- Why was Amalie nervous to tell Marcella that she'd shared her secret?
- Why didn't Amalie want to say exactly why she had shared Marcella's secret with Katie?
- What might have happened if Marcella didn't want to accept Amalie's apology?
- Should we ever keep secrets if someone is being hurt or in danger?

SKILL PRACTICE

Using the round-robin method, go around the table and ask students how they would practice each skill, giving every student a chance to answer one question. Skill practice can be adapted to allow students to answer in pairs or write their answers on scratch paper.

How Would You Practice Forgiveness If:

- Your friend didn't invite you to their party?
- Your classmate accidentally breaks your new birthday present?
- You get extremely angry with your friend and yell at them?
- You embarrass your brother by calling him by his nickname in front of his friends?
- Your teacher forgot to let you be the line leader after they'd promised?
- Your sister repeatedly takes your modeling clay without asking?
- Your teacher loses her temper with you and later apologizes?
- Your friend says something unkind to you and hurts your feelings, but apologizes?
- A friend breaks a promise to play basketball because their chores aren't finished?
- Your caregivers were late to pick you up from school, and you were the last student there?

ADDITIONAL ACTIVITIES

- Ask students to draw a picture about "What Forgiveness Looks Like to Me." Ask students to share and describe their pictures with the group.
- In pairs, ask students to interview one another about when they had to practice forgiveness or ask for forgiveness. If time allows, ask one or two students to share their experience with the group if they are comfortable.

CLOSING CONSIDERATIONS

Forgiveness means a person can acknowledge the hurt and still move ahead and give the other person another chance. Forgiving someone does not mean we excuse what they did or have to continue a friendship or relationship with them. Forgiveness is a choice to let go of our anger or disappointment and replace it with more positive feelings that bring us peace. It's important to remember that not everyone deserves our forgiveness; you get to decide whether someone deserves a second chance.

Ask students to summarize the content of this session's lesson into a single sentence. Students will then consider how they will practice forgiveness throughout the week. In pairs or groups of three, students may share their answers. If time allows, a few students may share with the whole group.

"WOULD YOU RATHER?" GAME

Playing the "Would You Rather?" game is a fun and engaging activity for students to develop their critical thinking skills. Students will reflect on their experience, evaluate their options based on their preferences, and reflect on the opinions of others, providing a different perspective and strengthening their sense of connection to one another.

WOULD YOU RATHER?

Copy and cut out the questions for small groups to discuss, or have each person stand in the center of the room and move towards one side or the other to show their vote for either option as the facilitator reads the questions aloud.

WOULD YOU RATHER FORGIVE SOMEONE AND GIVE THEM ANOTHER CHANCE OR NEVER TRUST THEM AGAIN?

WOULD YOU RATHER BE FORGIVEN FOR A MISTAKE OR WANT THE OTHER PERSON TO REMAIN HURT AND ANGRY?

WOULD YOU RATHER GIVE YOURSELF FORGIVENESS AFTER MAKING A MISTAKE OR STAY MAD AT YOURSELF?

WOULD YOU RATHER FORGIVE SOMEONE WHO HAS WRONGED YOU OR FIGHT THEM?

WOULD YOU RATHER ASK YOUR FRIEND WHY THEY WERE UNKIND TO YOU OR ASSUME THE WORST AND NOT TALK TO THEM?

WOULD YOU RATHER TRULY FORGIVE SOMEONE OR BRING UP THEIR MISTAKE EACH TIME YOU'RE UPSET WITH THEM?

30-MINUTE GROUPS: LIFE SKILLS

perseverance

[*PERSEVERANCE: sticking to a purpose or an aim; never giving up on what one has set out to do; try, try again; persist.*]

MIND MAP

On the board, draw a mind map and ask students to consider the meaning of *perseverance*.

30-MINUTE GROUPS: LIFE SKILLS

ASCA® STANDARDS

- **B-SMS 5.** Perseverance to achieve long and short-term goals.
- **B-SMS 2.** Self-discipline and self-control.
- **B-SMS 4.** Delayed gratification for long-term rewards.

DIRECTIONS

In a small group format, complete a brief check-in with your students. Ask them to share a highlight and lowlight for the week or check in using the weather to represent their emotions. In a large group format, you might ask for a thumb up if they're feeling good, a thumb in the middle if they're feeling okay, and a thumb down if they aren't doing well. Review the Group Expectations before asking students to share their knowledge of the topic from the previous week. Together, review the Mind Map. Then, read the Lesson Introduction and ask the Circle Time Questions before reading the Story Time and asking the Discussion Questions. Students can work in pairs to craft their responses or share with the whole group. Complete the Skill Practice, "Would You Rather?" game, and Additional Activities as time allows. Be sure to complete the Closing Considerations with each lesson. During the final session, ask students to complete their post-group survey.

LESSON INTRODUCTION:

Perseverance is when you have a strong will to keep going and never give up, even when things are tough. It's like when you're trying to learn a new skill, like riding a bike, and it takes lots of practice to get it right.

If you want to learn another language, be great at a sport, or learn something complicated, you'll need to use your perseverance. That means you should keep trying even if you feel discouraged or face obstacles. Break the task into smaller chunks and pace yourself over many days or months to make it easier. If you keep pushing forward and don't give up, you'll eventually be able to do it.

CIRCLE TIME QUESTIONS

Ask students to reflect and share their answers to the following questions with the group. Larger groups may need to be broken into smaller groups to give students ample time to share their answers and deepen the conversation.

- When have you had to work really hard to get something right?
- What are some words you might say to yourself to keep going when you're ready to quit?
- What advice might you give to encourage someone who is struggling to learn something new?

STORY TIME

Hand out coloring sheets and crayons or markers to students to work on while the facilitator reads the story, if desired.

The Language of Friendship

Rosaline immediately noticed that her new school smelled different than her last school. This school smelled sweet, but her last school had always smelled of broccoli. She was excited for her first day but nervous too because she didn't know anyone or understand the language.

The principal led Rosaline down a long hallway and stopped at a big wooden door with a glass panel in the front. Rosaline could already see twenty sets of eyes on her before she'd even stepped into the class. The teacher and principal talked privately before the teacher said her name and waved for her to enter the room.

Rosaline took a deep breath and walked into the class. The teacher said something she didn't understand and then ushered her toward a desk next to a girl with glasses and short brown hair. The girl smiled at her and then said something she didn't understand.

Everything was confusing, with everyone talking around her, and she didn't know what they were saying. Her uniform suddenly felt itchy, and the fabric was too stiff. She thought, "How am I ever going to fit in?" The rest of the day was a blur with new foods, new people, and all-new everything.

The next morning, Rosaline's excitement from the day before had worn off, and now she was nervous about going to school. She put on another too-itchy uniform and made the short walk to school. When she got to class, she was surprised to see the girl with short brown hair smiling at her. The girl introduced herself to Rosaline in Rosaline's native language. She said, "Hi! I'm Elia. It's so nice to meet you." Rosaline was stunned and thought she might cry with excitement. She suddenly felt less alone.

Elia had gone home the night before and looked up a simple greeting to welcome Rosaline, but she wanted to say more. Elia thought Rosaline was so cool; she had stickers on her notebook of Elia's favorite bands—she could tell they were meant to be friends. But being friends meant they would have to find a way to communicate beyond a simple greeting.

During their lunch break, the girls went to the library to check out language books and recordings to practice learning the other's language. The progress was slow, and they practiced for months. Trying something new was awkward, and they each felt so silly trying to make the words come out right.

Rosaline and Elia often felt discouraged, but they kept trying and asked each other for help when they felt stuck. They would practice a little bit every day together and independently. Finally, after months of practice, the girls could have an entire conversation without pausing to look up a word. All of their hard work had paid off, and they'd each made a new friend and learned a new skill.

DISCUSSION QUESTIONS

- What motivated the girls to keep trying to learn the other's language even when they were discouraged?
- What strategies did they use to learn the languages?
- How did their determination to persevere help them reach their goal?
- What obstacles did they have to overcome in order to learn the language?

SKILL PRACTICE

Using the round-robin method, go around the table and ask students how they would practice each skill, giving every student a chance to answer one question. Skill practice can be adapted to allow students to answer in pairs or write their answers on scratch paper.

How Would You Practice Perseverance If:

- While you are wearing rollerblades, you fall down more than you stand up?
- You are the only skilled player on a basketball team?
- Your caregiver asks you to help your little sister ride her bike without her training wheels?
- Math is your worst subject, and your teacher asks you to study harder?
- Your friend asks you to smoke even though you know it isn't safe or healthy?
- You have only one week left to finish your science project and you have lost all interest?
- After an argument, your brother is making it difficult for you to say that you are sorry?
- Your grandmother has a hard time hearing, and you need to repeat things multiple times?
- After school, many classmates continue to pressure you to skip your homework and play with them?
- You are not allowed to go outside until you have finished the Saturday morning chores?

ADDITIONAL ACTIVITIES

- Divide students into groups of three. Ask them to develop a commercial selling "perseverance." The commercial should include reasons why perseverance benefits others and why the lack of perseverance can be problematic.
- Ask students to write a letter or journal entry about how they are going to work on something that they cannot do very well, for example, math, throwing, hitting, or catching a ball, being kind to a little brother or sister, etc. Ask students to describe how they intend to practice "perseverance" to help overcome their problem.

CLOSING CONSIDERATIONS

Perseverance requires self-control to keep going. Many skills require us to keep trying even when things are tough. We can keep pushing forward when we break tasks into larger chunks, use positive self-talk, and ask for help.

Ask students to summarize the content of this session's lesson into a single sentence. Students will then consider how they will practice perseverance throughout the week. In pairs or groups of three, students may share their answers. If time allows, a few students may share with the whole group.

"WOULD YOU RATHER?" GAME

Playing the "Would You Rather?" game is a fun and engaging activity for students to develop their critical thinking skills. Students will reflect on their experience, evaluate their options based on their preferences, and reflect on the opinions of others, providing a different perspective and strengthening their sense of connection to one another.

WOULD YOU RATHER?

Copy and cut out the questions for small groups to discuss, or have each person stand in the center of the room and move towards one side or the other to show their vote for either option as the facilitator reads the questions aloud.

- WOULD YOU RATHER TRY TO SOLVE A BIG MATH PROBLEM ON YOUR OWN OR ASK FOR HELP BEFORE YOU TRY IT?

- WOULD YOU RATHER PRACTICE AN INSTRUMENT FOR 15 MINUTES EVERY DAY OR NOT BOTHER TRYING TO LEARN AN INSTRUMENT?

- WOULD YOU RATHER GIVE UP ON LEARNING TO PLAY A SPORT YOU WANT TO LEARN BECAUSE EVERYONE ELSE IS BETTER OR KEEP TRYING?

- WOULD YOU RATHER QUIT WHEN YOU'RE BORED WITH YOUR HOMEWORK OR TAKE A BREAK AND THEN FINISH IT?

- WOULD YOU RATHER THINK KIND WORDS TO YOURSELF WHEN YOU'RE TRYING SOMETHING DIFFICULT OR THINK MEAN THINGS BECAUSE IT DOESN'T COME EASILY?

- WOULD YOU RATHER GET IN TROUBLE BECAUSE YOU SKIPPED YOUR CHORES OR ASK FOR HELP?

> **It's not that I'm so smart.
> It's just that I stay with problems longer.**
> ALBERT EINSTEIN

PERSEVERANCE

Final Group Session

LAST SESSION:
Directions & Overview

This final session is recommended, but optional. You may conclude the group during the final lesson topic if time does not permit this final session.

Directions: This final session is more relaxed and carefree, allowing students to spend time with one another and process their feelings about the group's conclusion. Facilitators may provide structured games or allow students unstructured time together.

Post-Group Expectations: Many students will have grown accustomed to meeting with you and will need reassurance about what support will be available after the group's conclusion. Be sure to review the protocol for meeting with you once the group has concluded.

Pre- and Post-Group Survey: Ask students to complete the post-group survey. Review the directions aloud. Discreetly ensure that all of the questions were answered when the forms are returned.

Certificate of Completion: Present each student with their own Certificate of Completion. You can have as much or as little fanfare around this experience as you would like. Playing a song and asking students to stand and clap for their peers creates lasting memories for the participants.

Group Completion Letter: Give each student their Group Completion Letter to share with their caregiver, notifying them that the group has officially ended.

Group Conclusion: Ask each student to share what, if anything, this group has meant to them. Model this activity by sharing your experience as the group's facilitator.

Note to Facilitators: If your district allows, concluding a group with a meal is often a fun experience for the students. If you are unable to purchase a meal with the district budget, perhaps students could bring their lunches. Be sure to have caregiver permission and be familiar with student's allergies before providing students with any food.

THE RESOURCES IN THIS BOOK ARE AVAILABLE FOR YOU AS A DIGITAL DOWNLOAD!

Please visit **ncyi.org/downloadable-resources** to access the downloadable resources.

Enter the code below to unlock the resources.:

LIFESKILLS545

SMALL GROUP ACTION PLAN GUIDE

GRADE LEVEL
The curriculum is ideal for 2nd through 8th grade students.

GROUP TOPICS
Kindness
Patience
Respect
Gratitude
Responsibility
Honesty
Friendship
Compassion
Forgiveness
Perseverance

10-12 Group Sessions — 30 MIN

CURRICULUM & MATERIALS

Curriculum:
Use this Life Skills Workbook to facilitate your groups.

Materials:
Copies of surveys, coloring sheets, and "Would You Rather?" game. Crayons, pencils, and scratch paper.

ASCA® STUDENT BEHAVIOR STANDARDS 15

B-SMS 1.
B-SMS 2.
B-SMS 4.
B-SMS 5.
B-SMS 6.
B-SMS 7.
B-SMS 8.
B-SS 1.
B-SS 10.
B-SS 2.
B-SS 4.
B-SS 5.
B-SS 6.
B-SS 8.
B-SS 9.

NUMBER OF STUDENTS AFFECTED

Small group is ideal for up to six students. Fewer students if goals are related to behavioral issues.

Life Skills can be used for classroom lessons.

PERCEPTION DATA

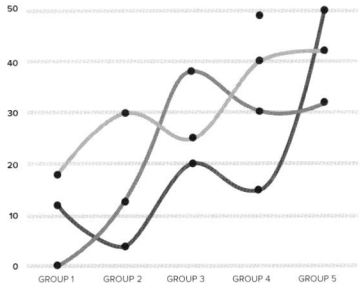

Use Life Skills survey data to create a visual representation of their progress using their pre- and post-group data.

OUTCOME DATA

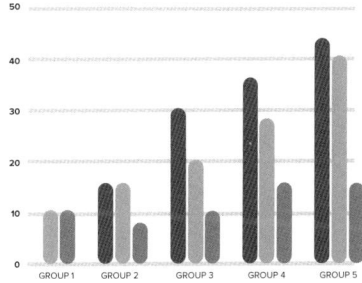

Use achievement, attendance, and behavior data to measure the progress of your students. Compare pre- and post-group impacts.

30-MINUTE GROUPS: LIFE SKILLS

LIFE SKILLS GROUP PERMISSION FORM

Greetings, Caregivers of: _____,

This form invites your student to attend a Life Skills group. Our counseling department offers various services, including class lessons, small groups, and individual sessions with students. There are lots of reasons we invite students to attend groups. We invite students who might need help connecting with their peers, help with skills to manage conflict or big emotions, to improve their grades, or simply because we think their involvement will allow them to be more successful in their education journey. Your student is not in trouble, and being part of this group is meant to be a positive time for all attendees.

This group will focus on building life skills related to kindness, patience, respect, gratitude, responsibility, honesty, friendship, compassion, forgiveness, and perseverance. Small groups are a fun way for students to learn valuable skills and connect with their peers.

We will meet for approximately thirty minutes during the school day ____ times per week. I will work with your child's teacher to select an appropriate time that minimizes interruptions to their learning. When the students have completed all the group sessions, they will receive a Certificate of Completion.

I am excited to be working with your child! Please don't hesitate to contact me with any questions or concerns.

Warm regards,

Please complete and return by: _____

Student's Name: _____

Teacher's Name: _____

☐ YES, I agree to allow my child to attend the Life Skills Group.

☐ NO, I do NOT agree to allow my child to attend the Life Skills Group.

_____
Signature of Caregiver

LIFE SKILLS GROUP EXPECTATIONS

CONFIDENTIALITY

In our group, we will keep what we talk about confidential. Confidentiality means keeping something a secret and not telling anyone else about it. We know that some things are private, and not everyone needs to know about them. However, because we are a group, we can't promise that everyone will keep your secrets, so please be mindful of what you share with the group. If you share that you plan to hurt yourself or someone else, or that someone is hurting you, I will have to break our confidentiality rule to keep you safe.

EVERYONE GETS A TURN

Everyone will have a chance to speak during each session.

LISTEN WITH RESPECT

We will give our full attention to the person speaking without raising our hands, thinking about what we want to say, or talking to others.

BE KIND

Disagreements are allowed, but we won't yell or call names to share opinions. We will use calm and safe hands and words.

CREATE YOUR OWN

_____

_____

Group Attendance Form

Group:_____ Day/Time:_____

	1	2	3	4	5	6	7	8	9	10	11	12
DATE												
	☐	☐	☐	☐	☐	☐	☐	☐	☐	☐	☐	☐
	☐	☐	☐	☐	☐	☐	☐	☐	☐	☐	☐	☐
	☐	☐	☐	☐	☐	☐	☐	☐	☐	☐	☐	☐
	☐	☐	☐	☐	☐	☐	☐	☐	☐	☐	☐	☐
	☐	☐	☐	☐	☐	☐	☐	☐	☐	☐	☐	☐
	☐	☐	☐	☐	☐	☐	☐	☐	☐	☐	☐	☐
	☐	☐	☐	☐	☐	☐	☐	☐	☐	☐	☐	☐

SESSION 1

SESSION 2

SESSION 3

SESSION 4

SESSION 5

SESSION 6

SESSION 7

SESSION 8

SESSION 9

SESSION 10

SESSION 11

SESSION 12

Group Attendance Form (Example)

Group: 5th Grade Lunch   **Day/Time:** Thursday @ 12:30

	1	2	3	4	5	6	7	8	9	10	11	12
DATE	3/2	3/9	3/16	3/23								
Jane/Ms. W's Class	X	X	X	X	X	X	X	X	X	X	X	X
George/Mr. Day's Class	X	X		X	X	X	X	X	X	X	X	X
Sami/Ms. Smith's Class	X	X	X	X	X	X	X	X	X	X	X	X
John/Ms. Lee's Class	X		X	X	X	X	X	X	X	X	X	X
Malik/Ms. Lee's Class	X	X	X		X	X		X	X	X	X	X
Prishna/Ms. Smith's Class	X	X	X	X	X	X	X	X		X	X	X

SESSION 1	Intro/Surveys/Group Rules and Norms/Discussed expectations/Played game.
SESSION 2	Kindness
SESSION 3	Patience
SESSION 4	Respect/They're starting to get along.
SESSION 5	Gratitude/Played game.
SESSION 6	Responsibility/M. shared about his dad.
SESSION 7	Honesty/The girls are now friends outside the group.
SESSION 8	Friendship/The did a great job practicing the Magic Formula.
SESSION 9	Compassion/S&G conflict outside of group resolved.
SESSION 10	Forgiveness/Reminded them that we only have two more groups.
SESSION 11	Perseverance/Plans for final group.
SESSION 12	Check-ins/Post-Group Survey/Process group experience & Certificates awarded.

Pre- and Post-Group Survey

My name is:_____

Date:_____

Life Skills Survey Pre-/Post-

Circle 👍 if the statement is **true** for you.

Circle 👎 if the statement is **NOT true** for you.

There are no right or wrong answers!

I can usually get along with almost anyone.	👍	👎
I am typically good at staying calm while waiting.	👍	👎
I usually use manners and say thank you.	👍	👎
I typically take responsibility if I do something wrong.	👍	👎
I am usually truthful even when I know I might get in trouble.	👍	👎
I am usually a good friend.	👍	👎
I am typically thoughtful of other people's feelings.	👍	👎
I usually forgive others when they make a mistake.	👍	👎
I typically want to help if I see someone in need.	👍	👎
I typically keep trying even if something is hard.	👍	👎
I have positive feelings about the group.	👍	👎

Anything else you would like to share about the group? Write it below.

_____

_____

Post-Group Survey Results
Life Skills Group Data

GROUP GOAL:

STUDENT STATEMENTS:

GPA Results
Increase the total GPA following group intervention for group participation by ____%

_____%

Attendance Results
Decrease the number of absences by ____% following group intervention for group participants

_____%

Discipline Results
Decrease the number of conduct referrals by ____% following group intervention

_____%

STUDENTS ATTENDED

NUMBER OF SESSIONS

OVERALL IMPROVEMENT
(See Formula Lower Right)

☐ Pre-Group % True   ☐ Post-Group % True

- I can usually get along with almost anyone.
- I am typically good at staying calm while waiting.
- I usually use manners and say thank you.
- I typically take responsibility if I do something wrong.
- I am usually truthful, even when I know I might get in trouble.
- I am usually a good friend.
- I am typically thoughtful of other people's feelings.
- I usually forgive others when they make a mistake.
- I typically want to help if I see someone in need.
- I typically keep trying even if something is hard.
- I have positive feelings about the group.

OVERALL IMPROVEMENT FORMULA

$$\left(\frac{\text{Post-Group Total} - \text{Pre-Group Total}}{\text{Pre-Group Total}} \right) \times 100$$

30-MINUTE GROUPS: LIFE SKILLS

Post-Group Survey Results (Example)
Life Skills Group Data

GROUP GOAL:

Reduce the number of discipline referrals by 10% for a group of six students who had more than three discipline referrals last year.

STUDENT STATEMENTS:

"I really like group."
"I learned how to share my feelings."
"I didn't have to feel embarrassed."
"I think I'm a better friend now."
"I know how to be patient now."

GPA Results
Increase the total GPA following group intervention for group participation by __5__ %

__5__ %

Attendance Results
Decrease the number of absences by __53__ % following group intervention for group participants

__53__ %

Discipline Results
Decrease the number of conduct referrals by __42__ % following group intervention

__42__ %

STUDENTS ATTENDED: 6

NUMBER OF SESSIONS: 12

OVERALL IMPROVEMENT: 41.94%
(See Formula Lower Right)

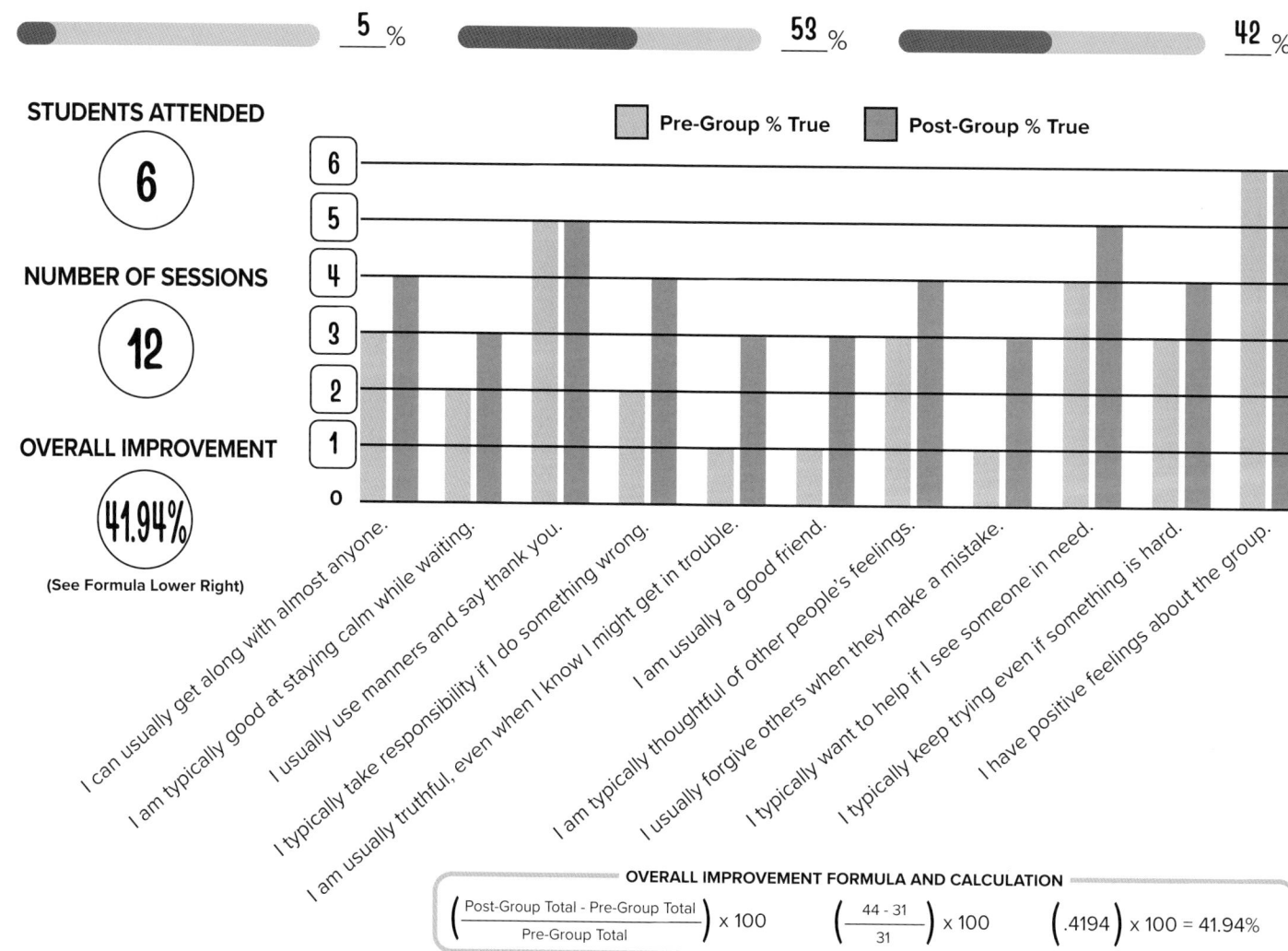

OVERALL IMPROVEMENT FORMULA AND CALCULATION

$$\left(\frac{\text{Post-Group Total} - \text{Pre-Group Total}}{\text{Pre-Group Total}}\right) \times 100 \quad \left(\frac{44 - 31}{31}\right) \times 100 \quad (.4194) \times 100 = 41.94\%$$

30-MINUTE GROUPS: LIFE SKILLS

30-MINUTE GROUPS
CERTIFICATE OF COMPLETION

YOU DID IT!

This Certificate is Presented to:

_____

For Participating in the **Life Skills Group!**

Facilitator: _____

LIFE SKILLS GROUP COMPLETION LETTER

Date:_____

Hello!

Today was the final session in our Life Skills Group, and we wanted to let you know that your student has been presented with a Certificate of Completion.

Over the past ten sessions, we have reviewed the following topics:

- Kindness
- Patience
- Respect
- Gratitude
- Responsibility
- Honesty
- Friendship
- Compassion
- Forgiveness
- Perseverance

I am still their counselor and will still be available to them as needed in the future. However, we will no longer be meeting every week. Please don't hesitate to contact me with any questions or concerns.

I am so proud of them and excited they were able to attend. Thank you so much for allowing them to participate in our Life Skills Group!

Warm regards,

_____
School Counselor

REFERENCES

American School Counselor Association. "Mindsets & Behaviors for Student Success: K-12 College- and Career-Readiness Standards for Every Student." American School Counselor Association. https://www.schoolcounselor.org/getmedia/7428a787-a452-4abb-afec-d78ec77870cd/Mindsets-Behaviors.pdf Accessed September 21, 2023.

ABOUT THE AUTHOR

Connect with Elishia at **thefeelingslady.com**

Elishia Basner is a former school counselor with a decade of experience aiding children and adolescents in navigating life challenges such as grief, loss, divorce, emotional regulation issues, and transitions. Elishia is passionate about helping schools become more resilient-centered and helping school counselors create comprehensive programs that align with the ASCA® National Model. Elishia has over 14 years of experience in counseling and education; she has a Master's degree in the Science of School Counseling and a Bachelor's degree in Psychology.

In her 14+ year career in the helping profession, she has done everything from working as a school counselor for a decade with every grade level from pre-k through college, in-home counseling with children at risk of removal from social services, managing a 24/7 women's crisis center, and teaching psychology to undergraduates. Elishia is an enthusiastic speaker who helps audiences connect to the information they need to help children thrive.

A Brief Look at Elisha's Workshop Sessions

De-Escalating Crises in the Classroom: Strategies 101

Learn how to better manage and diffuse a crisis with De-Escalation Strategies 101. In this session, you'll gain an understanding of why students lose control of their emotions and the best strategies for addressing difficult situations. You'll also learn proactive skills to help children of all ages develop regulation and coping skills to prevent future crises. With these tools, you'll be better equipped to ensure the safety and well-being of everyone in the classroom.

The Playlist for Creating a Trauma-Informed School

Do you wonder if your school is supportive of students who have experienced trauma? We understand that not all of our students have had the same experiences and many may be struggling in the Survival Brain, unable to access the Learning Brain. That's why it's so important to create an environment that promotes the learning brain, regardless of past trauma. See how you can help build a trauma-informed school atmosphere that is safer, calmer, and more conducive to learning for all students.

Empowering Educators: Unlocking the Keys to De-Escalation and Self-Regulation in the Classroom

When students' emotions are dysregulated, they can struggle to learn and distract those around them from learning. In this workshop, participants will uncover why students lose control and learn twelve scientifically-backed coping strategies that can be instantly implemented. Upon returning to your school, you'll be equipped with tangible skills to foster awareness, self-reflection, and connection with students.

ncyionline.org/speakers

About NCYI

National Center for Youth Issues provides educational resources, training, and support programs to foster the healthy social, emotional, and physical development of children and youth. Since our founding in 1981, NCYI has established a reputation as one of the country's leading providers of teaching materials and training for counseling and student-support professionals. NCYI helps meet the immediate needs of students throughout the nation by ensuring those who mentor them are well prepared to respond across the developmental spectrum.

Connect With Us Online!

@nationalcenterforyouthissues

@ncyi

@nationalcenterforyouthissues